IN
HIS
FOOTSTEPS

Other books by Ruth Carter Stapleton

The Gift of Inner Healing

The Experience of Inner Healing

Brother Billy

IN
HIS
FOOTSTEPS

The
Healing Ministry
of Jesus—
Then and Now

RUTH CARTER STAPLETON

Published in San Francisco by
Harper and Row, Publishers
San Francisco New York Hagerstown London

FIRST EDITION

Designed by Donna Davis

Library of Congress Cataloging in Publication Data

Stapleton, Ruth Carter.
    In His footsteps.

    1. Faith-cure. 2. Jesus Christ—Miracles. 3. Stapleton, Ruth Carter.
I. Title.
BT732.5.S754   231'.73   79–1767
ISBN 0–06–067516–0

79 80 81 82 83   10 9 8 7 6 5 4 3 2 2 1

CONTENTS

ACKNOWLEDGMENTS

I have been blessed in my spiritual pilgrimage with many friends, all of whom in their own way helped mold the ideas and spark the inspirational reflections in this book. It would take a small chapter to give them all proper recognition.

Gratitude demands that I specifically acknowledge those who helped develop *In His Footsteps.* This book is in reality more the result of a team effort than it is my own creation.

My faithful assistant and sometimes typist, Steve Carpenter, cheerfully bore the burden of translating my penciled first draft into typewritten manuscript.

My colleague in the inner healing ministry, Clifford Custer, contributed immeasurably to the development of each chapter.

Dr. W. S. McBirnie generously shared his biblical knowledge of the background material and made all the arrangements for these photos of my journey to the Middle East.

Roy M. Carlisle, my editor at Harper & Row, showed great skill and patience in his orchestration of the whole production.

Kathy Reigstad, also a member of the editorial team at Harper & Row, contributed her sizable writing talent in rearranging and sometimes rephrasing my thoughts, so that you, the reader, could have a more pleasurable and inspiring journey into the life of Christ.

INTRODUCTION

There is currently a renewal of interest in the Christian experience of being born again. But I feel that in a different sense *Jesus* needs to be born again. We need a fresh glimpse of his divine humanity. Our culture, and this generation in particular, lives as if history were optional. We clamor for a knowledge of our "roots" while denying, through ignorance and apathy, the relevance (and even existence!) of historical personages; tracing roots is a fad rather than a link with reality.

Jesus lived in Galilee as truly as I live in North Carolina. People met him, talked to him, listened to him, ate with him, were healed by him. Yet today we tend to view him analytically, objectively. We need instead to *experience* him; we must open our hearts to his Spirit until he becomes our dearest friend and companion. In our growing intimacy with him, there is no substitute for the Bible, particularly the four Gospels.

Jesus said to his first disciples, "Follow me." They did, and their experience of walking in his footsteps transformed their lives. The light that journey kindled in their souls has illumined the hearts of all who, through the centuries, believed their testimony and took that same pilgrimage of faith.

The purpose of this book is to make that original sacred journey come alive today through photography and inspirational reflection. The nine sections of black and white photos, arranged chronologically according to Jesus' life, represent significant events in his ministry. They and the color photos will take you on a visual journey to the dusty roads and centuries-old cities where people like you and me encountered the miracles of divine healing.

It is often difficult for us to believe that healing —whether emotional, spiritual, or physical—can happen, and even more difficult to believe it can happen to *us*. This photo reminder of Jesus' ministry of healing to real people in a real world may inspire your faith as the actual journey inspired mine. My sojourn in Biblical settings also sparked reflections on the meaning of Jesus' healing ministry for us today. The chapters of this book record those reflections, which are a journey in themselves—a journey of the mind and spirit through the Gospel records.

In His Footsteps is designed to work at two levels, visual and reflective, but not simultaneously; the photographic journey best precedes the reflective journey. The familiar Gospel stories on which the reflections are based may seem more alive to you when you can see in your mind's eye those places where Jesus lived and walked.

Let the Holy Land capture your heart as well as your eye. A deeper faith that comes from "being there," and an increased sense of God's omnipotent love, are this book's gifts to you.

B ut he, desiring to justify himself, said to Jesus, "And who is my neighbor?" Jesus replied, "A man was going down from Jerusalem to Jericho, and he fell among robbers, who stripped him and beat him, and departed, leaving him half dead. Now by chance a priest was going down that road; and when he saw him he passed by on the other side. So likewise a Levite, when he came to the place and saw him, passed by on the other side. But a Samaritan, as he journeyed, came to where he was; and when he saw him, he had compassion, and went to him and bound up his wounds, pouring on oil and wine; then he set him on his own beast and brought him to an inn, and took care of him. And the next day he took out two denarii and gave them to the innkeeper, saying, 'Take care of him; and whatever more you spend, I will repay you when I come back.' Which of these three, do you think, proved neighbor to the man who fell among the robbers?" He said, "The one who showed mercy on him." And Jesus said to him, "Go and do likewise."*

Luke 10:29–37

---

*Direct quotations from the Bible are taken from the Revised Standard Version. In some cases, however, I paraphrase the Bible rather than quote it directly.

AN
OVERFLOWING
CUP:

My Healing Ministry Begins

As a young Baptist housewife, emotionally broken and physically ill, I was introduced to Jesus as a living reality. He came to me as love. St. Paul describes such an experience as "the love of Christ shed abroad in our hearts by the Holy Spirit." I am not a great theologian as Paul was. I only know that a Jesus I did not feel worthy to approach, approached and embraced me. A God who in my youth seemed ready to condemn me for every sin I had ever committed became the loving, understanding Father that Jesus describes.

I was suffering at that time from lower back pains that required constant medication and a physician's care. I never asked for prayers for healing, yet over a period of six months I was healed. I sought love and found healing; others seek healing in Christ and find love. It makes no difference, because in his love is healing, and healing leads to love.

By being healed in Christ I found myself in a role to which I had not aspired—that of helping to heal others. I am by nature painfully shy before a group of people and I had no ambition to be a speaker or public figure. I just wanted to enjoy my home and circle of friends in Fayetteville, North Carolina. In fact, when I was first asked to give a short talk describing what God had done for me, I agreed, and then became so nauseated by fear that I could barely stand up to speak. But my fear was not as great as was my need to share with my friends what I had received from Jesus. That is all I ever wanted, and all I want today. I received no mystical calling; I was driven by no messianic ambition. I simply wanted to give to others the love of Christ as I myself had received it. I was caught up in a stream of divine compulsion.

My first real experience of God's redemptive love came at a retreat I attended. It was a spiritual awakening. I was in over my head—the singing, praying, and praising God were foreign to me. But even as my mind was systematically rejecting most of what was going on, my soul knew that I was in the right place with the right people to find what I was looking for. Deep personal, painful need often prompts the soul's recognition of God, because every other route away from pain—escape, rationalization, manipulation—have all led to a totally dead end. That was my condition, and I was beginning ever so slightly to believe.

The water really got deep during one of the retreat's evening prayer groups. Tommy Tyson, a giant of a man who laughed a great deal and seemed to enjoy religion the way some people enjoy a wonderful night out on the town, asked me to pray for one of the group members, a woman who was deaf. I panicked. I just did not do that sort of thing; but I knew I must. I did not know if prayer could heal sickness, but it might. And I could see that Tommy knew Jesus could heal her. Somehow I realized that he was right. I walked to the deaf woman and placed my hands over her ears, having once seen a faith healer (whom I believed at the time to be a conscienceless fraud) do that on television. I prayed. Where did my prayer come from? I believed every word I said.

"Lord," I prayed. "I know that you can heal this woman's ears. Please heal her now."

That was all, but that was enough. When I removed my hands the woman could hear—perfectly! My big friend Tommy Tyson was laughing. To him it was one more delightful bit of evidence that his living Savior was still in the business of healing people. I did not laugh. I wanted to cry. The impossible, which in a moment of prayer I had hoped, I had wished, I had somehow known could happen, happened. This is where faith is born and how it grows: we repeatedly step into an abyss, a bottomless void, and discover that the void has more solid footing than the earth of material or rational certainty.

Shortly after returning from the retreat where my immersion in holy love took place, I was invited to speak in a women's day of prayer program. The wives of servicemen at Fort Bragg who were planning the day of prayer received last-minute word that their scheduled speaker was unable to attend. They called my minister at the Snyder Memorial Baptist Church of Fayetteville, asking him to suggest a speaker on prayer. I occurred to him immediately. I had been driving him crazy, speaking to him about my new experience every chance I got. He was the only one I yet felt comfortable sharing everything about this new Christ with. I imagine that he was looking for some way to drain some of my excessive enthusiasm.

Present at the program was a chaplain, Merlin Carothers, who years later wrote the book *Prison to Praise*. The concept of praise was unknown to him when we first met; he was still imprisoned spiritually and very rigid emotionally—the typical joyless Christian. After I gave my day of prayer message he came up to me and said that he sensed something unique about it.

"I'm a Baptist," I said defensively. I was not about to reveal my secret to him. He was a starchy chaplain with gold crosses on his lapels broadcasting to all the world that he was commissioned by the army to dispense God to servicemen. I did not want to take on any army God-dispenser. Not yet anyway.

"The fact that you're a Baptist doesn't explain the difference I sense," he said.

I still did not feel free to confide in Merlin, but I invited him to a Monday night prayer group which I had started at my home. His curiosity overcame a deeply ingrained suspicion of anything even suggesting that emotion could be associated with God, and he came. The first night he was conspicuously stiff and proper in our circle of ten turned-on Christians. By the end of the evening, however, he was convinced that he was on the trail of some aspect of Christianity that he did not have. He started attending my Thursday morning Fort Bragg Bible class, which a Baptist chaplain had asked me to take over when he was sent to Vietnam. It was in that class that Merlin discovered he knew the Holy Spirit only by hearsay. His thirst deepened, so I urged him to attend a conference where people more mature in the Spirit than I was could minister to him. There he had his life-changing experience.

As a direct result of that transformation, Merlin knew he was not simply to console the sick or be a paid morale booster. He knew he must pray for those in his care. He invited me to accompany him when he prayed for the sick.

It is important to understand that neither he nor I had any particular desire to be healers. Nothing in our religious backgrounds prepared us for such a role. We adopted our ministry—or were adopted by it—because we followed a Living Christ, who walked the roads and streets of Galilee revealing a God of Love. His was the kind of love that always wants to heal, needs to heal, and has the power to heal.

One of the first young men we met in the military hospital was a paratrooper whose foot had been crushed by a piece of heavy equipment that had parachuted onto it. The foot was so badly mangled that the surgeons were unable to set it. My faith was small. But when Merlin asked me to pray with him for the boy I gently placed my hands on that severely smashed foot and asked God to heal it. Weeks later the orthopedic surgeons were amazed to find shattered bones healing correctly, though they had seemed hopelessly crushed.

So my ministry of healing began as Jesus' began, as every authentic expression of divine healing begins: with God's love flowing unselfconsciously from one whose cup is overflowing to one whose cup, in sickness, is empty. And when the empty cup becomes full, healing occurs.

THE SHEPHERDS' FIELD, BETHLEHEM. Our journey begins in the fields of Bethlehem. On the skyline can be seen the city of Jesus' birth. In ancient times these fields were probably the site of the gleaning by Ruth the Moabitess, an ancestor of King David and of Jesus. The shepherds, to whom the Christmas angels brought the news of the birth of the Savior, probably grazed their sheep in this vicinity.

THE SHEEP OF BETHLEHEM. Here Ruth holds a lamb in the fields where the shepherds watched their flocks and where the angels chanted the good news of Christmas.

THE CAVE OF THE SHEPHERDS, BETHLEHEM. Numerous caves where shepherds found shelter for themselves and their flocks can be seen in the areas in and around Bethlehem. Jesus was placed in the manger of just such a cave.

THE MARBLE-COVERED MANGER IN BETHLEHEM'S CHURCH OF THE NATIVITY. Jesus was born in a cave-stable under an ancient inn in Bethlehem and laid in a carved stone manger. Our journey takes us to the basilica constructed by Queen Helena, mother of Constantine, which eventually replaced the ancient inn. Constantine was the emperor and founder of the Christian Byzantine Empire which lasted over one thousand years.

And he said, "There was a man who had two sons; and the younger of them said to his father, 'Father, give me the share of property that falls to me.' And he divided his living between them. Not many days later, the younger son gathered all he had and took his journey into a far country, and there he squandered his property in loose living. And when he had spent everything, a great famine arose in that country, and he began to be in want. So he went and joined himself to one of the citizens of that country, who sent him into his fields to feed swine. And he would gladly have fed on the pods that the swine ate; and no one gave him anything. But when he came to himself he said, 'How many of my father's hired servants have bread enough and to spare, but I perish here with hunger! I will arise and go to my father, and I will say to him, "Father, I have sinned against heaven and before you; I am no longer worthy to be called your son; treat me as one of your hired servants." ' And he arose and came to his father. But while he was yet at a distance, his father saw him and had compassion, and ran and embraced him and kissed him. And the son said to him, 'Father, I have sinned against heaven and before you; I am no longer worthy to be called your son.' But the father said to his servants, 'Bring quickly the best robe, and put it on him; and put a ring on his hand, and shoes on his feet; and bring the fatted calf and kill it, and let us eat and make merry; for this my son was dead, and is alive again; he was lost, and is found.' And they began to make merry.

Luke 15:11–24

KEY
TO THE
RIDDLE:

The Power of Love

Naive romantics picture love as a ceaseless syrupy stream; cynics claim sardonically that it is a glandular illusion. It is neither. Love is the key to the riddle of human existence and the wellspring of peace, joy, and fulfillment. It is love that motivates a father to accept, welcome, and forgive the son who returns home after squandering an entire inheritance in debauchery and disgrace. Love is what prompts that father to bestow again the full honor of his household on the prodigal son and to celebrate his return, saying, "This my son was dead, and is alive again; he was lost and is found." God is like that father, said Jesus. God is love.

God is love and Jesus is love incarnate. Because he

came to reveal the true nature of God, everything that Jesus ever did was a visible expression of our all-loving Father. "If you don't believe my words," Jesus once said, "then believe because of what you see me do." He never questioned a person's past or present worthiness. Anyone who asked sincerely for help or healing received it, because a loving Father wants his children whole.

The dazzling sequence of events that is Jesus' life —his birth in a manger, the heroics and miracles of his brief life, his terrible death and spectacular resurrection—are natural consequences for the one person who knew perfectly how to give and receive love. The plot of his life was not developed by a God given to writing sensational scenarios. To love is to care, to care is to relate, and to relate is to communicate. Each facet of the life of Jesus is an object lesson in one of those three basic aspects of living. He healed not because it is the thing a messiah is expected to do, but because he cared for others.

And for the same reason there is no biblical hint that Jesus was ever ill. He cared for himself so much that he never restricted the life force which produces a perfectly functioning body and mind. We can and must abandon the idea that God played favorites with Jesus. It is just that because Jesus never suffered from self-contempt, his soul never lost contact with God. Therefore his body and mind remained attuned and whole. Jesus is not special in the sense of being singled out for special treatment by God but special because he defined humanity as it should be and then made that new definition a realizable goal for all. He became the prototype for a new humanity.

At the heart of every human ill lies a feeling of separation from God and one's fellow man. Instead of primal love perfectly forming the newborn baby's consciousness, there is primal trauma. Before our minds can express pain in words, we feel somewhat, or perhaps deeply, Godless. And to feel Godless is to feel loveless.

Our Godlessness/lovelessness expresses itself in a self-hate which is then projected on our other relationships. It is a vicious circle. I hate myself; therefore I hate others; therefore I hate myself more; therefore I hate others more. . . . And so we proceed into our own self-fueled hell. Yet Jesus cared enough to step into this circle of fire, to put it out even though it meant that he would himself be burned. "We love because he first loved us" is the biblical description of how the hate-self/hate-others cycle is broken by Jesus.

God's love is perfect in its beauty and cosmic significance, yet it is something we learn only gradually to imitate. On the path from self-contempt to self-love we make a broad, slow, sweeping turn, never a 180-degree about-face. What Jesus did is perfect, but my comprehension and integration of his love into my own life is less than perfect. In many respects, even after finding new life in Christ, I am still very much out of touch with love. I move through three mental states: reality, depression, and fantasy. When I am in touch with reality, I love God, I love others, and I love myself. But when I am out of touch, I either hate myself or I exalt myself and am apart from God. Depression makes me feel that I cannot get in touch with God, and fantasy makes me feel that I do not need him or others—both are deadly. We need the resurrection faith to help us believe in God, and we need hope to help us believe in ourselves as we slowly move along the path toward wholeness.

The first thing Jesus did after his resurrection was to seek out and help his broken, confused disciples. Then, after restoring their hope in themselves, he promised he would always be with them. Most of us need to see the whole series of events that surround the resurrection from a more human, practical perspective. Instead of looking up at actors on an elevated stage, we need to lower the stage to eye level and let the performers (the disciples) move among us in the audience. We need to take them home with us, invite them in the front door of our house, sit them down in our living room, have them eat at our breakfast table or sleep in our guest room. In other words, we need to let them become familiar to us. As friends they reveal the same emotional needs and characteristics we have.

When we become better acquainted with the disciples, especially Peter, their problems become almost uncomfortably familiar. Peter was quite sincere, but he did not know who on earth he was. Just before Jesus was arrested and executed, Peter responded violently to Jesus' observation that before the night was over he would three times deny that he even knew Jesus. His violent reaction was predictable. Anyone who has a weak or bruised ego finds it impossible to let down his guard and be exposed. (The encounter groups, so popular in the sixties, proved ineffective because they tried to force an encounter with our emotional weaknesses through confrontation. They did more harm than good in most cases. The groups in effect led a horse to bitter, stagnant water and then discovered that sticking his nose in did not make him drink.)

If criticism, even benevolent, constructive criticism, touches something we are not ready to face or exposes us to possible rejection, we draw on our arsenal of defense weapons: anger, tears, flight, condemnation of our critics. Before criticism can be accepted, the critic has to prove himself. That is why Jesus' return from the grave was so important. Jesus proved his point: Peter was weak and he *did* deny knowing Jesus. But Jesus also proved himself, and that is the crux of the story. Peter's weakness did not lessen Jesus' love for him. Jesus walked back into his life and, instead of saying, "See, I told you so," said,

"Peace be unto you; as the Father sent me into the world, so now I send you. . . ." How is that for unconditional love?

But Jesus knew that one moment, one peak experience, would not meet Peter's need further down the road. The disciple's self-respect was at rock bottom, and he had a long way to go before fully believing in himself. He would need repeated assurance of his self-worth, especially from Jesus. Self-respect, self-love, is not something we discover in one bright, exalted moment and then hold forever.

Jesus was perfectly attuned to the Source of all love. We, however, because of our imperfection and disconnection, cannot draw enough love from our communion with God; we need communion with others as well. But we need *true* communion, not only the frequent compliments or "warm fuzzies" we exchange—though these too can be expressions of real caring. The truly caring person is careful to let the significant people in his or her life know that they have worth and beauty. It is in the context of such a relationship, a friendship rich in affirmation and mutual support, that the necessary job of facing our imperfections can be successfully experienced. It was essential for Peter's salvation that he should say to Jesus from his heart, "I believe in you." It was just as important for his emotional development that Jesus say to him, as he did, "I believe in you."

In this kind of caring relationship real communication can take place. So much of our talking really communicates nothing of ourselves. Our words can be walls rather than windows. People learn things *about* us—for example, that I am Protestant, the President's sister, a healer, and an evangelist—but we rarely communicate our real identities. We fear that we will not be accepted if others see our real selves. Given that feeling, it takes a lot of "I believe in you" from others before *we* believe in ourselves. Your belief in me does not mean that you do not see my bad side; it means that you see beyond the bad to the me God is making into something perfect. A button people were wearing and handing out a couple of years ago carried this cryptic message: B P W M/G I T W M Y. It inevitably prompted the question, "What do all those letters stand for?" Came the answer, "Be patient with me. God isn't through with me yet." The proper response requires only two more letters: "OK." It is true that God is not through with me yet, and the me in the making demands constant undergirding.

On the lawn of a conference center I sat enjoying the sun and conversation with a friend. He was telling me of his struggle with and victory over alcoholism.

"I never had to join Alcoholics Anonymous," the giant of a man said. "I just quit six years ago and never went back to it."

"I think I know who helped you find sobriety," I said.

"Who?"

"Your wife, Julie."

Julie had a strong, deep love for her husband, far out of proportion to her small physical stature. I had often seen it expressed.

"You've got to be right," he agreed. "So many times I'd come home roaring drunk, vomit, break up furniture even, then fall unconscious on the floor. Julie and my two daughters had to haul me into bed and clean me up. Many times when I'd wake up the next morning, there was Julie looking over at me smiling and saying, 'It's nice to have the real you back.' "

There was a lot of love, a lot of caring, behind that wife's affirmation, and it finally communicated itself to this man's spirit. He began to love himself, eliminating the need to run to alcohol to hide from his self-contempt. It would be a dangerous mistake, however, to terminate his daily diet of tender loving care. He will need it until the day he dies. If he lost that love he would die inside, outwardly still alive, but brokenhearted.

The consistent caring of the Julies of this world does not come easy. There were times, I am quite sure, when Julie wept in frustration, others when she wanted to strangle her drunken husband with her bare hands. Love such as hers needs to be tough,

THE STEPS OF THE ROYAL PALACE OF SAMARIA. When Samaria was ancient Israel's
northern capital, these steps led to the Royal Palace.

Photo by W. S. McBirnie.

CHURCH OF THE NATIVITY, BETHLEHEM. Ruth and fellow pilgrims examine reminders of the past in Bethlehem's Church of the Nativity, built during the Byzantine Empire.

THE JORDAN RIVER NEAR CAESAREA PHILIPPI. It was in this river, pictured here near its source, that Jesus was baptized by John.

Photo by W. S. McBirnie.

MOSAIC OF JESUS, MARY, AND MARTHA. This beautiful mosaic adorns the Church of Mary, Martha, and Lazarus in Bethany, built to memorialize Jesus' raising of Lazarus.

Photo by W. S. McBirnie.

CHURCH OF THE TRANSFIGURATION, MT. TABOR. This church was built on what is thought to be the site of Jesus' transfiguration.

determined, and patient—results are rarely immediately fruitful. It asks us to believe, believe, believe, when there is so little in ourselves and others to believe in. St. Paul says that such divinely determined love "outlasts everything." I would paraphrase that by saying this kind of love out-performs everything as a healer of the human spirit. But such love has to put up with and overlook a lot in the process.

How does one come by this kind of love? Some people, having received caring from others, just naturally pass it on. Others have tasted the unconditional love of Christ directly, by spiritual contact with Jesus. For them, giving what they receive is a reflex action. The majority of us come by it a slower, harder way. We are pressed to our limit. We think we have no more to give, but the will says "I can," and the mind says "Lord help me." And somehow, from deep within us, our God-self born of the Spirit stretches and grows and does what we did not think it could, like an athlete pressed to the limits of his ability who rises to previously unachieved heights of performance. Spiritual growth often comes from facing the impossible, and finding out at the very last moment that, by God's grace and our will, the thing *can* be done. In extreme situations, I can give a measure of love that only a moment before I did not even have. Such a breakthrough increases self-love, both of the giver and of the receiver.

21

Just this kind of opportunity to stretch my heart was thrust upon me only months ago. A young woman from a nearby city came asking for counseling at a time when I was ready for help myself. I was emotionally exhausted. The pressures and demands of developing a retreat center, speaking to get funds for it, meeting the press, and fending off the curious —all this while sharing my heart with the interested and the spiritually needy—had left me feeling totally depleted. When I looked at the woman who presented herself to me, I did not know whether to laugh or cry. Her disheveled black hair shrouded most of her face, though I could see her eyes, the eyes of a frightened, caged animal, peering through a few parted strands. She was dressed totally in black: black plastic boots, black skintight pants, and a bulky black sweater.

"Ruth, I need your help," she said in a controlled voice.

"You poor child; you really do," I thought. "Let's sit down and talk," I said. I led her to one of the easy chairs in my bedroom at HOLOVITA, our new retreat center. I could sense her uneasiness, so I did not try to launch into a discussion of her problems immediately. I told her I was glad she had come for help and that I was sure she would find the answers she was looking for.

As she began to speak in earnest, she brushed her hair to one side with her hand, as though she were drawing back a curtain. The story she unfolded made me lose some of my confidence that her problems would be easily solved. She was a drug addict and had been actively involved in witchcraft. Her multiple emotional wounds were deep and serious. She suffered from chasms of depression as black as her appearance. Afraid of life, death, other people, and many of her own emotions, she was seriously considering suicide. Her physical condition had gravely deteriorated through drug abuse and what seemed to be hypochondria.

"Jesus," I thought, "you had better give me the grace of a saint. I'm going to take this mangy, lost puppy in, because I think I love her; I'm sure I do."

Every day she came to me for counseling. At first it did little more than reinforce my initial analysis that she was an emotional mess. Her first substantial breakthrough took place during the first weekend retreat she attended at HOLOVITA. Most of the participants were prominent, wealthy people from Houston, the women tastefully dressed and coiffured. It was fascinating to watch my shaggy girl in black timidly mingling among them.

The climate was one of warm love and sharing, and only a few hours after the weekend had begun, people became aware that this was no ordinary church conference. That indefinable chemistry of concern and Christ's power started eating away at walls of reserve and doubt. By Sunday morning the people sat in a circle openly sharing how they had met Christ as a living reality, while others told of emotional and spiritual healings. There were many glistening eyes and tear-streaked faces. One of those faces was new to the group—it had previously been hidden behind a curtain of hair. My young friend had gotten a haircut; she was coming out from behind her mask. It was eloquent body language.

The face I saw at last was quite lovely. Her eyes still retreated downward when she was spoken to, but there was less fear in them. I had initially dreaded the burden she would be, since we had almost nothing in common. I need not have worried. I was given a love for her from somewhere, from Someone, and it does not matter that her healing is ever so gradual. She is being healed, and that is all that matters to me. Like the father with his prodigal son, God has welcomed and accepted her, and offers her his unconditional love.

That shattered vessel, being repaired piece by piece by the Holy Spirit, often blesses me. Sometimes she lives at HOLOVITA for weeks. No job is too menial for her; without complaint she does anything she is asked to do as well as many necessary things she is not. "I just want to serve Christ," she insists, "and since you led me to his peace, I serve him by serving you." I am humbled by the love she shows. The one who said he had come to heal the bruised and brokenhearted has made a pathetic creature a beloved daughter.

THE WILDERNESS OF JUDEA. Our expedition progresses to the wilderness of Judea, where John the Baptist lived. Later Jesus, following his Baptism, spent the forty days of his fast here.

FISHING IN THE SEA OF GALILEE.

THE WELL OF JACOB (NOW CALLED NABLUS), NEAR SYCHAR IN SAMARIA. Here Jesus had the most important recorded conversation of his ministry. Dug by Jacob's sons about 1700 B.C., the well has held water ever since. In Jesus' day the curb was above ground, but has slowly been covered by the eroding soil from nearby mountains. A building was constructed by the Russian Orthodox Church to protect the well, one of the most clearly authentic holy sites in the Holy Land.

THE POOL OF BETHESDA, JERUSALEM. The ancient pool of Bethesda, after which great medical centers and hospitals the world over are named, is now found in the lowest reaches of the ruins of a great medieval church. It is here that Jesus challenged a sick man's self-pity with the words, "Wilt thou [really] be made whole?" and then healed him.

After he had ended all his sayings in the hearing of the people he entered Capernaum. Now a centurion had a slave who was dear to him, who was sick and at the point of death. When he heard of Jesus, he sent to him elders of the Jews, asking him to come and heal his slave. And when they came to Jesus, they besought him earnestly, saying, "He is worthy to have you do this for him, for he loves our nation, and he built us our synagogue." And Jesus went with them. When he was not far from the house, the centurion sent friends to him, saying to him, "Lord, do not trouble yourself, for I am not worthy to have you come under my roof; therefore I did not presume to come to you. But say the word, and let my servant be healed. For I am a man set under authority, with soldiers under me: and I say to one, 'Go,' and he goes; and to another, 'Come,' and he comes; and to my slave, 'Do this,' and he does it." When Jesus heard this he marveled at him, and turned and said to the multitude that followed him, "I tell you, not even in Israel have I found such faith." And when those who had been sent returned to the house, they found the slave well.

Luke 7:1–10

BELIEVING
IS
SEEING:

The Faith Factor

Faith is a little appreciated, rarely understood presence in our society. Many people look upon it as religious wishful thinking, a naive sort of wishing-will-make-it-so mentality. That it is not. Wishful thinking is simply bringing to the surface the desires of the subconscious mind—powerful desires that can do a great deal to dictate or change a person's life, either for better or for worse. Courses in positive thinking seek to harness the potential of wishful thinking through the processes of affirmation and positive planning. I am not belittling the value of wishful thinking; it can be useful for personal improvement. But wishful thinking is not faith.

Our ability to reason is a characteristic and significant aspect of our humanness. But there is something in all of us that occasionally allows us to transcend that aspect of our human nature. It ranges from the perception (at the most obvious level) that the harmony of radiant pinks and reds on the incandescent clouds of a sunset is beautiful and that the smashed face of an accident victim is not, to the sublime perception of the God and Father of our Lord Jesus Christ. None of these perceptions is open to reasoning dispute; they just *are.* There is within everyone a soul capable of knowing these things and of perceiving God's power. There is within each of us the capacity, by making contact with that part of ourselves created "in the image of God," to know and do God's will. It is that capacity which Jesus singled out in the centurion for honorable mention. The soldier knew beyond dispute— without doubt—that Jesus could, if he would just speak the word, heal the gravely ill servant he so deeply loved. The centurion's soul somehow knew. It had "evidence of things not seen," to use the phrase found in the eleventh chapter of Hebrews, the great faith chapter of the New Testament. What faith teaches us is not that "seeing is believing," but that believing is seeing.

The disciples knew that faith was somehow the secret of Jesus' power, and that they themselves needed more faith. So they did what so many people mistakenly do: they asked him to increase their faith. To their request Jesus responded, "If you have faith the size of a mustard seed, you can say to that sycamine tree, 'Be cast into the Sea of Galilee over there.' And it will be done." What did he mean? Simply this: use what faith you have and the little will become more. It is significant that Jesus compared the power of faith with a mustard seed. Seeds are alive and have tremendous growth potential. That is what he wanted his disciples to realize. If we do not use what we have, allowing it to grow, we lose what we have. Unfortunately, this is one of the principles of life. (And it is the reason why so little faith is in evidence in the church.)

On one of Jesus' visits to Jerusalem, at the pool of Bethesda, his attention was drawn to the face of one of the many anguished invalids surrounding the pool. A paralytic, the man had been incapacitated for thirty-eight years. Jesus looked at him and read the man's heart. He knew that for years the man had come daily to the Bethesda pool, waiting for his chance to roll into the water and be healed. Early in his years of vigil, he probably fantasized about that moment of healing. Perhaps he saw himself plunging into the roiling spring, feeling the surge of life through his body, then climbing out onto the porch and standing up. Everyone, he imagined, would gasp in amazement as he walked home. People who knew him would turn and stare; others would rush up to him and exclaim, "You're walking! How did it happen?"

Hundreds of times he must have pictured the great event, but years of frustration and discouragement had reduced the bright dream to a dreary, hopeless shadow. He was carried to Bethesda now more out of habit than hope. Jesus saw something more than discouragement in the man's spirit, however—something so painful that the man himself was not in touch with it. Jesus knew that his pathetic soul was a house divided against itself. Consciously, the man wanted to be healed. Subconsciously, he did not. But Jesus also saw that his years of suffering had driven him to the edge of faith. He was ready to say "yes" to wholeness instead of "yes, but no."

Approaching the paralytic, Jesus asked, "Do you want to get well?" (It is significant that Jesus went to only one of the many invalids at the pool. Divine guidance showed him that that one man was ready; the others evidently were not. Our human analysis cannot reveal when prayer for healing is right and when it is premature. Only God's spirit can know this.)

"I can't," the man answered in despair. "I'm alone. I haven't anyone to help me get into the water. When it moves someone else plunges in before I have a chance."

Life breathed on life in that moment. Something in the eyes of the tall stranger with the Galilean accent made the man want to kneel before God. He felt some sacred though stagnant pool within himself stir and well up as living water.

"Rise up," said the angel of healing who had moved on his soul. "Roll up your sleeping pad and go home."

The healed man went to the temple, knowing that he must thank God for his new limbs. He spotted Jesus among the worshippers and went to him.

"Now that you are well, don't sin as you did before," Jesus instructed him, "or something even worse might happen to you." Jesus understood that as much as the man had hated his paralysis, part of his mind felt he did not deserve to walk again. Guilt had led to a self-contempt that sentenced him to life without limbs. "Don't sin as you did before," meant, "Don't let guilt overcome you again."

The crucial need of that lame man was to feel worthy to receive healing, to sense a recognition of worth emerging out of a relationship. Just as emotionally healthy parents love their children and want the best for them, regardless of how good or bad their conduct may be, so God our Father wants us to have healing and wholeness. That is why Jesus said, "If you, being evil parents [when compared with the perfect good of God] give good things to your children, how much more will your heavenly father give good things to those who ask?" In simple terms then, the man at the Bethesda pool felt like an evil, naughty boy who for reasons unknown and unstated must be punished. So Jesus let his soul know without words, beyond words— for the soul speaks in ways that existed before tongue and lips were formed, and it will continue to speak when death reduces the vocal cords to dust— "you are loved, you are worthy to walk." The man heard with his soul and walked.

Jesus transformed the man by communicating his love and compassion. A truly great communicator does not talk superficially, or just emotionally; he or she draws from deep within the soul a force that has life-changing effects on others. That is what happened at the Bethesda pool. The depth of the love communicated to the lame man neutralized his self-hatred and kindled faith in his doubting spirit, making healing possible. The person we call a healer is one whose soul is deep in faith, love, and selfless service, and who—like our Lord Jesus—can convey that to those sick in body and soul.

On the first day of a week-long conference in the Midwest, I was approached by a woman wearing braces on her legs and back and supporting herself with crutches. She told me that she had been paralyzed since she was six years old. She had attended a school for crippled children, and then, as a young woman, she met a man who wanted to marry her in spite of her condition. They had three children.

"Mrs. Stapleton, will you pray for my healing?" she asked.

I knew the time was not yet right. I needed spiritual preparation and I wanted the support of people who would join their faith with mine.

"I will pray for you," I said, "but now is not the time. Sometime during the week we'll get together. I'll let you know when."

Four days later I was leading a prayer group that included the woman. I led them in a discussion on the power of the Holy Spirit. As the hour progressed, I felt the time was right to pray for her healing. I told the group about her earlier request and suggested that we now honor it. Before praying, I said that if anyone felt doubt about God's power to heal, the most helpful thing that person could do was to leave. One person asked to be excused.

I stood beside the woman and invited the nine others to gather around her as we prayed. Some went to their knees; others stood with their hands on her shoulders. Placing my hands on her head, I prayed that in the name of Jesus Christ, and through his power, she might be healed.

The woman began to moan as sharp pain shot through her legs and back. There was an involuntary twisting and moving of her limbs and hips. The pain was so great that she started crying. I was concerned; something was happening, but what? The petitioners became spectators as the Spirit moved upon her withered, twisted legs and feet. One misshapen foot began to move from its radically pigeon-toed position to that of a normal foot. Long-unused muscles were drawing the complex bone structure of both feet into proper alignment. We cried as we massaged her legs and feet. We could feel the healing presence of Christ and see his healing touch. At last all her pain subsided. She sat staring at her straightened feet, then stood up slowly, leaned forward, and touched her toes. "Look at that!" she exclaimed.

Someone went to tell her husband and children the good news. When he arrived, her husband looked down at those legs and feet no longer held in braces. She was standing erect and whole. "I don't believe it!" he said in joyously believing tones. Then he took her in his arms as they wept together.

The next day she knocked on the door of my room. When I opened it, the radiant woman of the day before was gone. She was dejected and crestfallen. "What's the matter?" I asked, puzzled.

"Oh, Ruth, I'm so confused. I thought I wanted to be healed, but now I don't think I do." She buried her head in her hands. "I can't bear the idea of taking responsibility for myself. I've been taken care of all my life." Then she paused. "And what frightens me most is that I still want the drugs I took for my pain.

The pain is gone, but I still want those pills." She was addicted.

"Your healing has just begun," I said. "You have some way to go before you are healed totally. But God began your healing yesterday, and he will complete it, if you will to be whole."

"I guess I do, Ruth, but I'm so frightened."

I told her that the will to live as a whole person was barely alive within her, that she needed to nurture it and carefully bless it. I told her to stay in close contact with friends who knew Christ's love and who loved her.

She stood up. "I want to live," she said. "I'm going to make it, because I *do* want to live."

The inner enemy was in full retreat, though it had not been completely destroyed. In the months that followed, her offensive against darkness grew in strength. She was released from her drug addiction. She was still walking, physically and spiritually, because she regained her will to live.

A CHURCH IN CANA OF GALILEE. While attending a wedding feast in Cana, Jesus performed his first miracle, memorialized now by a church constructed over a well. A waterpot of ancient design, such as would have contained the water-turned-wine, is pictured.

THE CHAPEL OF THE SERMON ON THE MOUNT, GALILEE. Set well back from the Sea of Galilee is the small mountain where it is believed Jesus took his disciples to recite his famous Sermon on the Mount, which some have called "the Constitution of the Kingdom." This chapel was a gift of the Italian government fifty years ago.

THE CHAPEL OF THE SERMON ON THE MOUNT.

THE COLONNADE OF SAMARIA, ANCIENT ISRAEL'S NORTHERN CAPITAL. The Roman administrative center of Palestine, Samaria was flourishing at the time of Jesus. The city was first founded by Omri more than 800 years before Christ.

THE SYNAGOGUE, CAPERNAUM. The ruins of this synagogue, dating to the second century A.D., probably stand on or near the site of the synagogue in which Jesus preached.

Now when Jesus returned, the crowd welcomed him, for they were all waiting for him. And there came a man named Jairus, who was a ruler of the synagogue; and falling at Jesus' feet he besought him to come to his house, for he had an only daughter, about twelve years of age, and she was dying. . . .

While he was still speaking, a man from the ruler's house came and said, "Your daughter is dead; do not trouble the Teacher any more." But Jesus on hearing this answered him, "Do not fear; only believe, and she shall be well." And when he came to the house, he permitted no one to enter with him, except Peter and John and James, and the father and mother of the child. And all were weeping and bewailing her; but he said, "Do not weep; for she is not dead but sleeping." And they laughed at him, knowing that she was dead. But taking her by the hand he called, saying, "Child, arise." And her spirit returned, and she got up at once; and he directed that something should be given her to eat. And her parents were amazed; but he charged them to tell no one what had happened.

Luke 8:40–42, 49–56

CHAPTER FOUR

TWO SHALL BE AS TEN THOUSAND:

Unity in Faith

Why are some people healed through prayer while others remain unaffected? That question troubled me for many years. The inconsistency made God seem terribly unfair. Surely God does not play favorites, but what other explanation is there for the varying results to sincere prayer for healing? Some people are content to say, "We can't know the answer to that question; it's a mystery. It's just the will of God that some people be healed and others remain ill." That answer has never satisfied me. The God and Father of our Lord Jesus Christ, the Father of us all, is perfect love; he doesn't will sickness any more than he wills sin. Both sickness and sin are the result of being out of touch with God.

The real answer lies in the healing ministry of Jesus. There was no inconsistency there. Every single person who went to him for healing was cured. But if we carefully review his ministry, we find it reveals some basic principles which, if followed, produce healing. If the principles are ignored, healing is blocked. It is not God who is inconsistent in his mercy; it is we who are inconsistent in our application of the principles of healing.

The importance of faith for successful healing is discussed in a previous chapter. Without our faith, the power of God is short-circuited in its flow to the pathological body, mind, or spirit. An extension of the principle of faith is the principle of unity within faith. What can be accomplished by two people united in faith is geometrically greater than that which one person, or two people praying independently, can accomplish. The concept is expressed scripturally as, "And one shall be as a thousand and two shall be as ten thousand." It provides the correlation between two statements in the second chapter of Acts: "And they were all together with one accord" and "There were added that day [to the Christian community] about three thousand souls." That kind of abundant power of conversion could not have been manifested by the Holy Spirit if unity of faith had not been present. The ultimate source of physical energy is nuclear fusion; the ultimate source of spiritual energy is the fusion of person with person, and person with God.

In 1974 I was given the opportunity to go to Indonesia as part of a healing team. While in that steamy, tropical land I saw material poverty and spiritual riches such as I have seen nowhere else. At a Sunday evening service in Solo, Java, we invited anyone who wished to have prayer for healing—physical, emotional, or spiritual—to come down to the chancel. In the center aisle a cluster of worshippers leading a woman blind from birth moved toward the altar. While I prepared to pray for the woman, her friends made a circle around her, united in their love for her and Christ; they were sure he would heal her. As we all prayed, she began to speak excitedly.

"She says she can see!" said our interpreter, with equal excitement.

I put two fingers before her once sightless eyes and asked her, through the interpreter, how many fingers she could see.

"Two," she responded without hesitation.

I walked to the very rear of the sanctuary and asked the same question with all my fingers extended. From over 100 feet away she answered, "Ten."

Everyone in that circle of faith wept for joy. They had come to Christ in unity, believing that he would heal their friend. And seeing their faith, he had said to her, "Be thou made whole."

There is unfortunately a negative application of the principle of unity as well. A group of people united in opposition or antagonism to the idea of divine healing and prophetic ministry can greatly hamper the work of the Holy Spirit. Jesus himself encountered such opposition in his own home town. Of Jesus' ministry in Nazareth Matthew sadly observed, "And he did not do many miracles there because of their unbelief." It was not that God did not want to perform his mighty deeds there, but that the resistance of the Nazarenes blocked the healing flow. His hometown frustration stands in stark contrast to the miracles of Capernaum: the healings of the centurion's servant, Peter's mother-in-law, the paralytic, Jairus' daughter, and the woman with the hemorrhage.

The powerful negative impact of collective doubt is one of the reasons Jesus told people not to discuss their healings. "Tell no one," he frequently said. Collective antagonism can plant the seed of doubt in the mind of the healed person. If the doubt is not removed, the negative suggestions and atmosphere can cause the illness to return. Genevieve Parkhurst, a pioneer in the healing ministry, suggests that if one is going to pray for a person with an often terminal disease such as cancer, it is better to pray for them before the prognosis gets out and the circle of friends has the object of prayer already dead and buried in their mind. People tend to believe the word of medicine more than the Word of God, and their collective doubt in the case of a terminal disease often blocks healing.

Jairus, an official of the synagogue in Capernaum, came to Jesus imploring him to save the life of his critically ill only daughter. "At this moment she is very near death," Jairus said. "Please Jesus, come quickly."

Jesus agreed to accompany the man, but his lack of urgency was disconcerting to Jairus. Before they arrived at Jairus' home they were met by a friend bearing the sad news of the daughter's death. Jesus' words cut through Jairus' grief: "Stop your fear. Just believe, and she will be restored."

Mourners had already gathered to pay their respects to the little girl when the men arrived. "Stop all this commotion," Jesus said. "The child isn't dead. She's asleep." The mourners, having seen the corpse for themselves, scorned his diagnosis.

Sensing disbelief in the home, Jesus asked everyone to leave, with the exception of his three closest disciples—Peter, James, and John—and the girl's father and mother. Then he walked over to the child's pale and waxen body, the vacant house of her soul.

Leaning over the child with the tenderness of a mother he said, "Talitha cumi," or "Little lamb arise." Her soul returned; the glow of her flesh was restored.

Turning then to the parents, he said to them, "Tell no one what you saw happen here." His concern was not for his fame but for the child. He had first instructed the parents to give her food. Her physical well-being established, he then urged them to remain silent about her recovery, lest her sensitive soul, and theirs, be tainted with the scorning doubt of others.

Soon after I was born of the Spirit I found myself needing to protect a miracle from collective doubt. My son Scotty, then thirteen, was riding his bicycle to the grocery store. Coming out of an alley onto the street he rode in front of a car that was pulling out of a parking space. The driver was looking over his left shoulder, checking for oncoming traffic. He stepped on the accelerator to enter the flow of traffic without looking straight ahead first. He hit Scotty and sent him flying headlong onto the pavement. One of the witnesses to the accident called an ambulance while someone else called my husband.

I was in the library at home, wondering why Scotty was taking so long, when my husband appeared at the door. "Get a babysitter," he said. "Scotty has been hit by a car. I think he's all right, but they've taken him to the hospital."

My husband rushed to the hospital immediately; I stayed to arrange for someone to take care of Michael, my youngest child. When I got into the car I was still crying, but in the midst of my tears, I remembered one of the spiritual instructions I had received at a recent conference—give thanks to God for everything. I began to say aloud, "Jesus, thank you for Scotty's accident. Thank you for everything that's happening to him. Thank you, Jesus; thank you, Jesus; thank you, Jesus." I had stopped crying, but more than that, I had lost my apprehension; I had absolutely no fear for my son. I *knew* he was going to be all right.

When I arrived at the hospital, my husband's face was etched with anguish, his eyes filled with tears. Our minister and the attending physician were with him. The doctor said, "Mrs. Stapleton, your son is in a very serious and regressive condition. He was conscious when he arrived, but is unconscious now. I want you to know we have done what little we could. Now we must just wait. He has less than a 50-50 chance of recovery."

I found myself consoling him and my husband. "Don't worry," I said. "Scotty is going to be all right. God isn't going to let him die."

"Do you want me to call members of the congregation?" my minister asked anxiously.

I knew that faith healing was not something he

then believed in, nor did most of the members of his congregation, so I said, "No, don't tell anyone, please." I knew that God was healing my boy and that doubters could somehow interfere with that process. The Holy Spirit let one of Christ's most ignorant new disciples in on this secret to successful miracle prayer.

"Just get me a cot, so I can stay by Scotty's side," I said to the doctor. "Everything is going to be all right," I repeated with a smile.

The three of them thought I was in shock, but I was not. I was in the Spirit.

After they left, I sat down beside Scotty's bed. He lay motionless, his eyes closed, his face pale; but I was unperturbed. Twenty hours passed before Scotty opened his eyes. "Who are you?" he asked in obvious confusion.

I stood up and took his hand in mine. "I'm your mother," I said.

"Who am I?" he further inquired.

"You're Scotty Stapleton."

"What happened to me?"

"You were in an accident. You were hit by a car and are resting in the hospital."

"Can I get out of bed?"

"Not yet, honey. You have to rest awhile."

"Then can I read some comic books? Would you get me some comic books?"

"Sure I will, honey; I'll go right now," I said, holding back my tears of joy until I left the room.

When I returned a few minutes later with the latest escapades of Batman, Robin, and Spider Man, Scotty looked up bright-eyed and smiling.

Not many people were in on this miracle—just enough to make it work. And that is how it should be, according to divine strategy. The atmosphere of faith must be protected from the contamination of group doubt as much as possible to enable God to do the mighty works that the sick and broken of his world so desperately need.

THE HOME OF ST. PETER, CAPERNAUM. Authenticated by decades of archeological work as the home of St. Peter, this scene of several of Jesus' healing miracles later became a shrine, though several successive building foundations have been identified. We cannot get much closer than this to the actual times and places associated with Jesus. His great healing ministry in Galilee was centered in Capernaum, and he lived here for a time.

THE STAR OF SOLOMON IN THE SYNAGOGUE, CAPERNAUM. On the heavily decorated stones of the synagogue in Capernaum (second century, A.D.) can be seen the star of David, the ancient symbol of Israel.

MAGDALA, HOME OF MARY MAGDALENE. The ancient village of Magdala, uncovered by archeologists, was not far from Capernaum.

THE RUINS OF MAGDALA. The home of Mary of Magdala (Magdalene) was in this town on the Sea of Galilee. After being delivered from demon possession by Jesus, she became one of his foremost followers, going even to the cross where she stood with the mother of Jesus.

A VILLAGE IN GALILEE. Not far from Capernaum, this modern village houses Jewish settlers.

And Jesus went away from there and withdrew to the district of Tyre and Sidon. And behold, a Canaanite woman from that region came out and cried, "Have mercy on me, O Lord, Son of David; my daughter is severely possessed by a demon." But he did not answer her a word. And his disciples came and begged him, saying, "Send her away, for she is crying after us." He answered, "I was sent only to the lost sheep of the house of Israel." But she came and knelt before him, saying, "Lord, help me." And he answered, "It is not fair to take the children's bread and throw it to the dogs." She said, "Yes, Lord, yet even the dogs eat the crumbs that fall from their master's table." Then Jesus answered her, "O woman, great is your faith! Be it done for you as you desire." And her daughter was healed instantly.

Matt. 15:21–28

BLESSINGS IN DISGUISE:

The Working of God's Will

Jesus began his miracle ministry on a very human note. He and his disciples had accepted an invitation to a wedding party in Cana, a small town nestled in the hills about fifteen miles southwest of Capernaum. In the rather austere life of the Galilean peasant, one of the few opportunities for light-hearted fun was a wedding celebration. The festivities preceding a wedding usually lasted the better part of a week. For the wedding in Cana evidently more friends and relatives showed up than had been expected by the hosts, the parents of the groom. No doubt word had gotten out that Jesus of Nazareth, whom many already believed to be a mighty prophet, was going to be one of the guests. Perhaps more people came to see this charismatic leader than to celebrate the wedding itself. As a consequence, the wine, which was the standard beverage at every social gathering, ran out.

(I can sympathize with the host in this situation. Last year when my son Scott was married, his uncle, President Carter, was among the invited guests. What normally would have been a relatively quiet family affair turned into a media event. Several hundred more people were in attendance than would have been there had the President of the United States not been present. It was an honor to have him but we ran low on food, punch, and patience because of the crowd.)

The miracle at Cana may have been Jesus' first recorded miracle, but it was obviously not the first demonstration of his supernatural powers. When Mary, who was also at the wedding, heard of the shortage of wine, she knew immediately how to solve it; she did not hesitate to go to her son and request that he remedy the situation. She already had ample evidence that the fruit of her womb, the Son of God, could somehow come to the host's rescue. I would even hazard the guess that she said to herself, "I think he ought to do something, since he's the reason they ran out of wine in the first place." And he did.

There has been a lot of misunderstanding about

the conversation recorded in this story. Jesus' response to his mother's request, "Woman, what have I to do with you; my time has not yet come," is misleading. There is a harshness in the translation that the actual words do not convey. A more accurate translation would be, "My lady, you have nothing to worry about. The time just hasn't been right to act." He was not putting her off; he was not saying, "I'm not going to perform a miracle for you, so leave me alone," which the popular translation implies. We can be sure of this because he went from his mother and performed the miracle she requested—not because she requested it, but out of compassion.

Both the first of Jesus' three great temptations in the wilderness and his first recorded miracle have to do with the same thing—the lack of food or drink. In the wilderness, when Jesus was without food, Satan suggested that he turn one of the stones into bread. Jesus refused, though it would have been natural for anyone with his powers to succumb to the temptation to manipulate things to satisfy his creature comforts, as well as to impress people into following him. But he refused to sell his soul short: "Man shall not live by bread alone but by every word which proceeds out of the mouth of God," he told Satan. "I want God's will," was his message. "I want to be a servant of my Father, not the master of my fate." He could accept his empty stomach as being just as blessed as a full one, if it was the will of God. With this settled in his heart and soul he was ready to go out into our selfish world, a world that crowns anyone, even a tyrant, who can satisfy its physical needs and wants.

What has all this to do with healing and wholeness? A great deal. We are not fully effective as channels of blessing and healing because we lack the quality Jesus had when he was confronted with the domestic problem in Cana and with his own hunger in the wilderness. We lack divine neutrality, which is the capacity to face a situation empty of all emotion save the desire that the highest and best be done. At each challenge of need or pain, Jesus could move into a realm devoid of human wants and requirements. God was his meat; God was his drink; God was his pleasure, his safety, his satisfaction, his all. It did not matter that he or anyone else was hungry, thirsty, or lacking in some other way. All that mattered was God. That neutral state left him receptive to God's perfect wisdom and absolute compassion. Whatever God dictated could be done. The channel cleared, water could be delivered to the desert, ready to bloom.

In Cana, the water became wine. Mary told the servants, "Whatever my son instructs you to do, do it." He had them fill six large pots with water —a total of about 200 gallons. Then, with the same creative force that formed the universe, Jesus breathed on water and made it wine.

That kind of power could not have manifested itself without divine neutrality, whose function is very like that of the vacuum in an incandescent light bulb. If air is not pumped out of the bulb, the filament burns up the moment the power is turned on. But in an atmosphere-free environment, the power causes the filament to glow, giving off light. The freer we are of our earthly wants—the less earthly atmosphere of anxiety and selfishness we have—the more God is able to use us to light up life. If his power passes through us without such a sacred surrounding vacuum, we are destroyed by the power we seek to use.

In one of my early Fayetteville Bible classes, a young woman named Sally, whose mother had been seriously ill for many years, repeatedly asked the class to pray for her mother's healing. We did so, but there was no improvement in her health.

One afternoon Sally drove out to my house, asking that we two pray privately. As we sat facing each other, I took her hand and said, "Sally, you need to release your mother. Give the whole thing to Jesus, and start thanking God that she's healed, that it's done, even though the healing hasn't yet been manifested. Let's do it on our knees." Rarely did I invite anyone to kneel. In this particular situation, however, it seemed right—an expression of submission to and worship of a good and glorious God.

A couple weeks later Sally came to my home again. "I have a problem," she said. "I don't feel like I care anymore whether Mother gets well or not."

It was apparent that this feeling was a source of guilt, so I explained that her lack of concern was a result of her prayer to release her mother to God's care, and that she had no reason to feel guilty. She should instead give thanks that her years of worry were over. She had given her mother to God; she could give him her worry as well.

It came as no surprise to learn that soon after our second talk Sally's mother began to improve. In just a few months she was completely well. It had all begun with an act of grace that left a daughter worried about not being worried. When Sally realized that even her worry was now in God's hands, her anxiety-free love allowed the healing of Christ to shine on her mother.

"Have no anxiety about anything, but in everything by prayer and supplication with thanksgiving let your requests be made known to God. And the peace of God, which passes understanding, will keep your hearts and minds in Christ Jesus." That is the scriptural formula for divine neutrality. The water of our humanity is waiting to be changed into the wine of Christ's divine provision. "Do whatever he says," Mary told the servants. We too are God's servants. Our responsibility is to "do whatever he says." If we are open to God's will we, like those servants at the marriage celebration in Cana, will become witnesses to the miracles of God through us.

God's will sometimes puzzles us; it seems at cross-purposes with our needs. Yet ultimately God's answers to our prayers for healing can always be reconciled with his infinite love for us.

Why did Jesus treat the Canaanite woman he met in Tyre with contempt and verbal abuse when she asked him to deliver her daughter of demons? At first he refused to even address her, so she turned in desperation to his disciples. They suggested that Jesus send her away; since she was a Canaanite, one whose ancestors had lived in Palestine before it was conquered by the Jews, she wasn't Jewish enough for them. Hers was mixed blood: she was both a "pig," the pejorative term then used by Jews to describe Gentiles, and a "dog," the corresponding epithet for Jews. She lived in two worlds, belonging to neither, resenting both.

To her repeated beseeching Jesus finally responded, "It is not fair to take the children's bread and throw it to the dogs." This he said to expose the nerve of her bitterness, to bring her face-to-face with the root cause of her distress. He knew that he had to push her to the breaking point before she could cooperate with him in the healing of her daughter.

In all likelihood, the daughter's broken condition was in great measure influenced, if not actually caused, by her mother's bitterness. So it would have been cruel to heal the daughter only to send her back into the situation which had originally infected her soul.

The woman understood Jesus' message and, facing herself with fresh honesty, was willing to accept her "dogness" and humbly receive from him any crumb of blessing he would give her. She embraced Christ in faith, which allowed her to embrace herself, her *whole* self.

"O woman, great is your faith," Jesus exclaimed. "Your request is granted." In that instant, her daughter was healed.

When Jesus commanded, "keep on asking and it shall be given to you; keep on seeking and you shall find; keep on knocking and it shall be opened to you," he was reminding us that we are not always ready to receive his blessing. In the parable of the woman who wore down a judge by relentlessly begging him for a fair judgment, Jesus commends her persistence and says that we should emulate her manner in our petitions to God. It is not that our importunity can change God's mind. That would be a selfish and unrealistic outlook. It is rather that determined, repeated prayer ends in success because we ourselves change. A situation frequently looks different when exposed to the light of God's presence and, as in the case of the Canaanite woman, that light enables us to see ourselves more clearly. We then make the adjustment of attitude that is essential for God to act on our behalf.

Anyone who dares to ask God for help, and is sincere in his request, is asking for the exposure of everything within him that is blocking the hand of God. Many an alcoholic who seeks sobriety finds himself powerless to recover until, through enlightened counsel or Alcoholics Anonymous, the underlying self-hate is exposed. Most alcoholics go through the terrifying experience of "bottoming out" —of arriving at that point in life when all avenues of escape seem cut off. Then when the only remaining options are to commit suicide or commit oneself to God, they find sobriety.

A close associate of mine, a minister and counselor, had a friend who was an alcoholic living on one to two fifths of whiskey a day. As the men talked in the minister's study one day, my friend confronted the issue.

"Joe," he said, "you're an alcoholic." When Joe denied it my friend said, "You are giving me the privilege of buying your next fifth of booze."

"You can't do that; you're a minister," the man protested.

"Yes, I'm a minister, but you are a drunk, and until you recognize it and stop kidding yourself, you can't find sobriety. I want to help you find the truth about yourself as quickly as possible. That's why I'm going to buy your next bottle."

The man looked down at the floor. "All right," he confessed. "I'm an alcoholic. What do I do about it?"

Through the power of the Holy Spirit and the support of Alcoholics Anonymous he became and remained a sober man—but not until he was willing to acknowledge that he was a drunk.

In another case, an attractive young woman came to me for counseling, saying she wanted to "really live." Her young rebellious spirit was tired of trying to be a good Christian. It was clear to me that her help could only come through pain, and I knew what I had to tell her. Though my words would sound like her emancipation, they were an invitation to pain and suffering.

"Sally," I said, "if, as you have said, you don't see anything wrong with things like getting high on pot, getting drunk, or sleeping with men, go ahead. God won't love you any less, and neither will I. But I think you'll discover that you'll love yourself a whole lot less. And that isn't fair to you. But it's your decision, so feel free to do all the things you think will give you happiness." She was a bit bewildered by my advice. She had expected prohibition and gotten permission. But I knew it was permission to hurt herself.

In a few weeks she was back. She thanked me for having granted her the right to try her wings. She had discovered that the cup of selfish pleasure was filled with very bitter medicine. "I've been a fool," she could say of herself, and with that revelation came a fresh desire to serve God. She wanted to enter a convent. Though she never became a nun, she did take a step into divine freedom, and that, after all, is what she had been looking for. She just had to learn that she had been looking in the wrong place.

To a casual observer, my instruction to the young woman would have sounded as wrong as Jesus' insult of the Caananite woman sounded on the surface. Yet any event that helps open our eyes to ourselves and to our need to have God touch us in our brokenness with his healing hand is good. In both of the above instances, the goal was blessing, the vehicle pain. Pain and sorrow, the dark angels of God, are often the only messengers our hearts will hear.

While teaching the Fort Bragg Bible class, I came to know and love a young woman whose husband was on a tour of duty in Guatemala. She and their little daughter, Marie, had to remain in Fayetteville. While he was in Central America, Ed bought a beautiful parrot for his wife. He had to smuggle it in to her, because our government prohibits the importation of birds that can carry vermin infected with parrot fever, transmittable to humans.

Several weeks after Sarah received the parrot, Marie became ill. Laboratory tests confirmed that it was parrot fever. Sarah asked me to pray with her for her daughter. When we finished, I said, "I really believe God is healing Marie. Everything is going to be all right." Her doctor knew that Marie's best chance for survival was special treatment at Walter Reed Army Hospital, so the mother and child were flown there immediately, and Ed arrived on special leave.

As the parents sat beside their comatose child, they talked and prayed together. Ed had been an atheist, but his feelings of shock and guilt made him review his life. He came to know the Jesus his wife loved and faithfully served—the only one who could save his guilt-ridden heart.

Two weeks went by before I heard anything more. Then Sarah phoned me. "Ruth, I just called to tell you that Marie is all right now; she was healed. But not the way we expected. She died last night."

I was stunned. "But Sarah," I said in a tear-choked voice, "I was so sure she would be healed. What happened?"

"Ruth, you musn't feel that way." (She was consoling me!) "Marie is healed. She's whole now, and my husband has come to know Christ. I'm so grateful to Jesus for all he's done for Ed and Marie. Don't be sorry, Ruth. Don't grieve for me. All I ask is that you pray for Ed's family in Houston. We're on our way there for the funeral, and they don't believe in Jesus the way we do. They won't understand why I'm not crushed."

I promised to pray. After we expressed our love and said goodbye, I remained by the phone, weeping, but I was not grieving any longer. Mine were tears of grateful joy. We may not defeat death, but Jesus always does. We feel the human loss at the death of loved ones and feel a little less alive ourselves because we cannot touch or see them for a season, but deep within we know that our departed friends are never more alive than when they walk into eternity. Because Sarah had often sat at the feet of Jesus, because she "had chosen the better part which cannot be taken away," she could say from the depths of her heart at her daughter's funeral, "O Death, where is thy sting? O Grave, where is thy victory?" Thanks be unto God who has given us the victory through our Lord Jesus Christ.

THE SYNAGOGUE CHURCH, NAZARETH. In the lower part of a church in the home town of Jesus can be seen ruins of the early synagogue believed to be the place of Jesus' first sermon in Nazareth. Here Ruth contemplates that moment when the Isaiah scroll was read with such authority by Jesus.

THE BAPTIST CHURCH, NAZARETH. Ruth visited Nazareth's Southern Baptist orphanage, school, and church. Shown here with Ruth are officials and teachers of the church.

74

THE PLACE OF THE MIRACLE OF THE LOAVES AND FISHES. Holding fish from the Sea of Galilee and native "loaves" of bread, Ruth is at the very place where Jesus performed his miracle of the feeding of the five thousand.

THE MURAL OF THE MIRACLE OF THE LOAVES AND FISHES. Near the Sea of Galilee, this stone mosaic mural stands in the ancient church that memorializes the miracle of Jesus' feeding of the five thousand.

THE SEA JESUS LOVED. On the Sea of Galilee, Jesus stilled the storm and walked upon the water, and in its waters, those fishermen whom he called to be disciples cast their nets.

Therefore confess your sins to one another, and pray for one another, that you may be healed. The prayer of a righteous man has great power in its effects.

James 5:16

Be merciful, even as your Father is merciful. "Judge not, and you will not be judged: condemn not, and you will not be condemned; forgive, and you will be forgiven; give, and it will be given to you; good measure, pressed down, shaken together, running over, will be put into your lap. For the measure you give will be the measure you get back."

Luke 6:36–38

THE
ROOF
FALLS
IN:

Sin, Illness, Forgiveness, and Health

The thrill of witnessing physical healing—seeing the lame walk, the deaf hear—tends to overshadow the less visible healing of the soul that accompanies or underlies it.

A guilt that paralyzes the soul can express itself in the body language of immobile limbs. The subtle interplay between body and emotions translates, through the endocrine system, negative feelings into negative physical conditions. The seeds of hate, unforgiveness, and consequent self-hate, when sown deeply enough in the soil of one's subconscious, are often reaped as illness. When that is the case, the underlying guilt and self-hate must be identified and removed in a climate of faith and love before the person can be physically healed. "The prayer of faith will save the sick man . . . and if he has committed sins, he will be forgiven" (James 5:15).

A woman at one of my conferences had an eighty to ninety percent hearing loss, begun when she was four years old. She told me that she had asked many people to pray for restoration of her hearing, including two of the world's best-known faith healers, but no prayer had succeeded.

"Who spoke to you, when you were a very little child, in such an ugly way that you wanted to tune them out?" I shouted.

"That's easy," she replied. "My grandmother. She ruled our house. She sat at the head of the table and looked down her nose at us. She always spoke in French and insisted that we do the same. Because I couldn't speak it well, I hated it. When I refused to answer her in French she called me stupid. I hated her!"

"You will have to forgive her," I said.

"But I can't," she insisted.

After being led back to the repeated childhood trauma at the dinner table, through faith-imagination, she was finally able to express her anger to her grandmother. She confessed that she hated her enough to kill her. After that outburst, she was able to forgive her grandmother completely.

Then I placed my hands on the 67-year-old woman and prayed. In that moment her hearing was completely restored.

A ministry of healing that ignores the emotional and spiritual roots of illness is incomplete. It is important to remember, however, that God "does not deal with us according to our sins, nor requite us according to our iniquities" (Ps. 103:10). We bring disease and sickness upon ourselves, by violating deep spiritual principles and laws. Jesus often talks about the results of an unforgiving heart:

> Therefore I tell you, whatever you ask in prayer, believe that you have received it, and it will be yours. And whenever you stand praying, forgive, if you have anything against any one; so that your Father also who is in heaven may forgive you your trespasses (Mark 11:24, 25).

When Jesus was in Capernaum, where his popularity was greatest, the crowds that followed him numbered in the thousands. On one occasion, as he sat answering the questions of a group of suspicious, curious religious leaders, the street outside was a solid mass of humanity. People were clustered around the front door and at the windows, straining to hear or catch a glimpse of the wonder worker.

One citizen of Capernaum was a paraplegic who had been confined to his bed for years. He and his friends knew that his only hope of ever walking again was in Jesus. The four faithful friends carried the man on a rigid pallet to the house where Jesus was meeting. They found the crowd so densely packed that there was no possibility of bringing their lame friend into the presence of the Master. As they stood at the edge of the crowd pondering their dilemma, one of them had an inspired suggestion.

"Why don't we get up on the roof, take the tiles off above where Jesus and the other men are sitting, and lower Simon down in front of him. Then Jesus is sure to heal him."

The unroofers went to work. Dust and small shard began to fall on the heads of the gathering below, and none but Jesus took kindly to the baptism of faith. What were those crazy men up to? The faithful four lowered the pallet, gently letting out the length of rope equally at each corner so that their fraternal cargo would not be dumped out.

Jesus looked at the proud, excited faces of the men. They knew their friend was about to be healed. "And seeing their faith, Jesus said to the man, 'My son, your sins are forgiven.' "

The religious leaders furtively glanced at one another with looks of shock and disapproval. "Who does this crazy man think he is, forgiving this man's sins. God?"

Jesus could feel their negativity, and he knew what they were thinking. Turning to them, he said, "You take offense at my absolution of this man's sins. Which would be easier for me to say to him, 'I forgive you your sins,' or 'Be healed'? Now since you think it is more difficult to heal this humanly hopeless case, I'm going to show you my divine right to forgive sins by healing him."

With the bold authority of the one who once spoke the whole creation into existence, he said to the paraplegic, "Rise, take up your pallet and walk." It was creation revisited. The darkness of that man felt the glory of the first sunrise, the joy of Adam, formed of Eden clay and Holy Breath. Obedient to the voice of his Creator-Savior, he picked up his bed and walked.

"My son, your sins are forgiven . . . . Take up your pallet and walk." The link between sin, disease, forgiveness, and healing is obviously present, but it remains mysterious. Jesus is the only one who understands it completely, and the only one with the authority and power to deal with it effectively.

The end result of his ministry is wholeness of body, soul, spirit, and mind. In our present age, Jesus has chosen to work through us by his Holy Spirit. We are to reach out, as he did, to those who are afflicted. We are one antidote to pervasive guilt and poisonous self-hate in others. A Middle Eastern proverb says, "A friend is someone to whom you may go and pour out all the contents of your heart, chaff and grain together; knowing that with gentle hands he will take and sift it, keep that which is worth keeping, and with a breath of kindness, blow the rest away."

Jesus is the perfect embodiment of that kind of friendship. And once we have experienced him, it is our privilege and obligation to be that kind of friend to others. A person frequently remains trapped in self-contempt until he finds someone who knows Jesus and is therefore open and vulnerable—a friend who is willing to show his own personal weakness, his own badge of soiled humanity. A guilt-ridden person can let that kind of friend into his darkened world, to light the lamp of forgiveness.

A friend of mine came to me one evening, asking if I knew someone to whom she could confess her sins. I told her I would be glad to act as her confessor.

"Oh, I couldn't let you do that!" she protested.

"Why not?"

"You're too good. You've had too nice a life to hear my confession. I don't think you could stand it."

Of all my friends, this woman was one of the dearest. Though I had known her for years, she still held me at a bit of a distance. To her I was Mrs. Wonderful. I knew that to help her I had to expose

THE CITY OF DAVID. The ancient part of Jerusalem, known as the City of David, looks much as it did in Jesus' day.

Photo by W. S. McBirnie.

TEMPLE COMPOUND, JERUSALEM. This is one of several entrances to the Temple Compound in Jerusalem.

Photo by W. S. McBirnie.

GOOD FRIDAY CEREMONIES. Worshipers gather here at the Judgment Seat of Pilate before following the traditional Via Dolorosa to Calvary. The modern building pictured was erected on the foundations of the Roman Praetorium.

Photo by W. S. McBirnie.

THE GOLDEN GATE, JERUSALEM. Sealed off in the early Middle Ages, this gate in the city's eastern wall will be opened again when the Messiah comes, according to scriptural tradition.

Photo by W. S. McBirnie.

WINNOWING NEAR SYCHAR. The practice of winnowing (separating the grain from the chaff), here being done near Sychar in Samaria, was referred to by Jesus as symbolic of the Judgment.

Photo by W. S. McBirnie.

myself. I had to show her that I was not the paragon of virtue she imagined me to be. It was frightening to think of emotionally disrobing in front of her, but I knew I must. Confession is an essential element of the fellowship our Lord created. "Confess your faults to one another," James instructed the early Christians.

"I think I have just as much sin in my past as you do," I said.

"I don't believe it. What's the worst thing you have done?" she asked.

"I don't want to begin with the worst thing. I'll start with the first sin I can remember and we'll go from there."

I had never before shared so intimately with a close friend. To make things easier I dimmed the lights and we sat quietly for a moment. As I began to tell of every major sin I had committed, her eyes widened in amazement. She said nothing, but the point struck home. I had barely started on my adult years when she interrupted with, "That's enough! You are just as sinful as I am."

Having established that questionable virtue, she felt free to unburden her load of guilt on me. It was my turn to listen. She held nothing back. Her guilt flowed away like refuse in the mighty cleansing river of God's love. She was released from the paralyzing pain of self-contempt and could accept Christ's absolution.

An additional benefit we derived from the experience was a strengthening of our bond of friendship. We respected each other more, rather than less, after our act of mutual exposure.

To love someone for his or her virtues is easy, and demands no real spiritual commitment, but to love someone who is flawed by sin expands the soul. It allows us to imitate Christ and it binds our heart to our friends and to God. The Great Commandment tells us to love God with all our heart, and our neighbor as ourselves. I can think of no higher way to love a God of grace and mercy than by expressing his forgiving spirit toward a neighbor. In so doing, we increase our love for ourselves.

When I harbor personal guilt, the process works in reverse: my self-hatred, which is projected onto my neighbor, reflects a contempt for God.

One of the incidents John recorded in his gospel illustrates the festering nature of self-hatred. Jesus was speaking to a gathered throng in the outer, or Gentile, court of the temple—the Hyde Park of Jerusalem, where itinerant advocates of various movements and causes were permitted to preach. The audience was held spellbound by his eloquent and authoritative delivery until at the edge of the sea of attentive faces a commotion broke out. Angry Pharisees were pushing through the crowd with a young woman, whom they pushed in front of Jesus.

She was a harlot, with a pretty, painted, but fearful face. Her eyes were cast down in shame.

The group's spokesman said in disgust, "Teacher, this woman was caught in the very act of adultery." A murmur rose from the audience; people glared at the fallen creature. Venomous words turned the curious crowd to an angry mob. "The Law of Moses says that a woman guilty of such a crime must be stoned to death," the spokesman reminded her ominously. Of Jesus he asked, "What do you say?"

Jesus was sickened by their grotesque display of cruelty and hypocrisy. He knew the Pharisees hoped to trap him in the law, but he said nothing. Jesus knelt in silence and wrote something in the dust of the polished marble pavement, as the woman's captors badgered him for his response. What he wrote is not recorded, but one tradition says that it was these words of his Father: "I would have mercy rather than sacrifice" (Prov. 21:3).

Then he stood up and, with one sentence, stripped them of pretense. "Let the man among you who is without sin cast the first stone!" Shame and frustration welled up uncontrollably in them. They had been publicly humiliated by the one they had come to humiliate. In that moment, if they could have murdered Jesus with impunity, they would have. That being impossible, there was nothing for them to do but leave the scene of their shame as quickly as possible.

As Jesus knelt again to write they all stalked away, leaving him standing alone with the woman in front of the crowd.

Now Jesus turned to the accused woman. "Lady" —that was the word he used—"Lady, where are your accusers? Didn't any one of them condemn you?"

"No, sir."

"And I don't condemn you either. Go your way and sin no more."

Jesus' words, and his strong, tender eyes, lifted layer after layer from her heart. In him she saw what she had unknowingly been looking for—love. Always before she had seen lust, or contempt, or disgust. Here at last was one who knew what she was, and who loved her. She was free. She knew she would love, follow, and obey him as long as she lived. She felt neither shame nor bitterness but joy as she walked away through the crowd.

Probably no story in history gives more hope to the guilt-ridden and morally fallen than this one. It witnesses to the nature of God as total love and demonstrates that when he meets total brokenness, the result is forgiveness and blessing. It also shows that in the presence of such love, only the condemners are condemned; and that not by God but by themselves.

It was the Pharisees' own guilt and consequent self-hate that motivated them to assault and humiliate the harlot. What Jesus knew, because he understood the human spirit, was that they would have seen no reason to condemn the woman had they not first condemned themselves. His words, "Let the man among you who is without sin [guilt] cast the first stone," were right on target.

The only way out of such self-destructiveness is to accept the love Jesus embodies and then to forgive those we would otherwise scorn and condemn. In those for whom we feel the most contempt, we meet self-contempt. In forgiving them, we forgive ourselves. The moment I forgive the person I find it difficult to forgive, I embrace what Jung described as my "dark side"—that part of me that I do not want to see. Reminded of it in others, seeing it paraded in broad daylight, I am enraged—such wickedness is unforgiveable! But as long as I continue to deny its existence in me, and more importantly, refuse to embrace it, it drives me like some cruel demon.

A minister came to me bitterly claiming that some of his fellow ministers had accused him of not being Christ-centered. Some had even called him a heretic. He was furious and claimed that he was being victimized by men whose very faith he questioned. He hated, in his self-righteousness, his self-righteous colleagues. I asked him to consider if his tormentors might not be a reflection of weakness in himself. At first he thought the idea absurd, but after days of pain and prayer he saw its validity. He knew he had to forgive, and did, thereby forgiving himself. Not many weeks after this breakthrough, the same men extended to him their hand of fellowship. But even if they had not, the victory would have been significant. He had embraced his real enemy—himself. He had said to his dark side, "I don't condemn you. Go and sin no more."

THE ENTRANCE TO THE POOL OF SILOAM, JERUSALEM. In Jesus' day, a blind man came to this pool to wash from his eyes the clay that Jesus had used in the act of healing him. As one of the few sources of fresh water in Jerusalem, the pool was frequented by large crowds of people drawing their daily water supplies. These people witnessed this singular act of healing and spread the fame of Jesus far and wide. Opening the eyes of the blind by the touch of the Master's hand became a symbol of the enlightenment of those who are spiritually blind.

"SUFFER THE LITTLE CHILDREN TO COME UNTO ME." Children are the same the world over in their delights and in their response to loving attention. This little Arab boy is yet unaware of the great history of the Holy Land, but he understands kindness and love.

A NEWLY EXCAVATED AREA SOUTH OF JERUSALEM. In this area, archeologists are revealing the city of Jerusalem that Jesus knew so well. Several of Jesus' healing miracles occurred nearby.

THE CAVE OF JEREMIAH, JERUSALEM. According to ancient local tradition, this is where the prophet Jeremiah (600 B.C.) lived, and where he dictated Lamentations and his prophetic book to Baruch, the scribe.

ELISHA'S FOUNTAIN, JERICHO. Here the great prophet Elisha turned bitter (salty) water into sweet. The artesian spring still flows, now irrigating the fertile soil near Jericho—and cooling the feet of dusty and tired travelers. (The desert climate often sends the mercury zooming over 100 degrees.)

And when they came to the disciples,
they saw a great crowd about them,
and scribes arguing with them. And
immediately all the crowd, when they saw
him, were greatly amazed, and ran up to
him and greeted him. And he asked them,
"What are you discussing with them?" And
one of the crowd answered him, "Teacher, I
brought my son to you, for he has a dumb
spirit; and wherever it seizes him, it dashes
him down; and he foams and grinds his
teeth and becomes rigid; and I asked your
disciples to cast it out, and they were not
able." And he answered them, "O faithless
generation, how long am I to be with you?
How long am I to bear with you? Bring him
to me." And they brought the boy to him;
and when the spirit saw him, immediately it
convulsed the boy, and he fell on the
ground and rolled about, foaming at the
mouth. And Jesus asked his father, "How
long has he had this?" And he said, "From
childhood. And it has often cast him into
the fire and into the water, to destroy him;
but if you can do anything, have pity on us
and help us." And Jesus said to him, "If you
can! All things are possible to him who
believes." Immediately the father of the
child cried out and and said, "I believe; help
my unbelief!" And when Jesus saw that a
crowd came running together, he rebuked
the unclean spirit, saying to it, "You dumb
and deaf spirit, I command you, come out of
him, and never enter him again." And after
crying out and convulsing him terribly, it
came out, and the boy was like a corpse; so
that most of them said, "He is dead." But
Jesus took him by the hand and lifted him

up, and he arose. And when he had entered
the house, his disciples asked him privately,
"Why could we not cast it out?" And he
said to them, "This kind cannot be driven
out by anything but prayer."*

Mark 9:14–29

---

*Other ancient authorities add *and fasting.*

THE
DISCIPLINE
OF
PREPARATION:

The Effects of Prayer and Fasting

Jesus expected success in healing. He expected a miracle, says a popular religious slogan. He also had a vision of God and man which made that high expectation realistic. He did not know what it was to take on more than he could handle. His unblemished record of success is not matched by that of any of his disciples—then or now.

When Jesus came down from the mountain with Peter, James, and John after his transfiguration, he found the rest of his disciples waiting in frustration and defeat. A man had brought his son to them to be healed, and the disciples had failed. They were powerless to free the child from the force that held it in hell on earth.

Jesus turned to his followers and said, "Oh faithless and perverted generation. How long do I have to endure you?" This is the closest Jesus seems to have come to despairing of others. He had called the disciples to follow him because his Father had instructed it. But at that particular moment he was frankly disquieted by their incompetence. He did not expect perfection from them, but he *did* expect enough compassion for suffering humanity to enable them to deal with such situations of critical need.

Jesus then directed his attention to the boy. To the father he said, "If you can believe he will be healed, do it."

Despite his discouragement at the disciples' failure to help his son, the father felt hope well up in his heart when Jesus took control. "I believe, Lord. Help my unbelief."

What a beautiful, honest confession from one who had just encountered failure. Ancient prophecy about our Lord reminds us that "he will not break the bruised reed or quench the smoldering flax." He will breathe on the faintest ember of hope in the human heart, if we extend even a trembling hand out to touch him.

The father's faith was rewarded; Jesus addressed the demon with a frightening authority and delivered the boy. More alive than he had ever been, he walked into his father's grateful embrace.

This healing left the disciples troubled. They were happy for the boy and his father, of course, but they were very unhappy with themselves. "Why did we fail?" they asked Jesus.

"You failed," Jesus said, "because you were poorly prepared. Some spirits don't come out except after prayer and fasting."

Success in any endeavor demands preparation. Jesus made it clear from the beginning that anyone who wanted to follow him would have to undergo severe discipline. There simply is no such thing as discipleship without discipline. To make his point, Jesus said a builder would be foolish to begin construction of a house if he were unsure that he had enough materials to complete it. And he said that no general in his right mind would begin a campaign against an enemy army unless he had carefully studied the opposition and had determined that he had a superior fighting force. By the same token, Jesus wanted no one to follow him without having counted the cost—not just one-tenth of our time or money, but ten-tenths of our whole being.

An attempt at such total commitment inevitably leads the Christian disciple to the painful discovery that some situations are just too taxing. They demand more muscle than we have developed. To his frustrated disciples, Jesus said, in effect, "You are undertrained. You are poorly conditioned. You are like a group of enthusiastic novice joggers who decide to run a fast ten miles the third time you jog together, and then wonder why you collapse before running half the distance." Spiritual achievement demands conditioning. Fasting and prayer are among the spiritual exercises we can all benefit from.

Prayer is almost universally praised, if less widely practiced, as a means of growth and grace. Fasting, on the other hand, is often thought to border on the fanatical. In a society that extols practicality and levelheadedness, while showing a discouraging absence of both, totally abstaining from food is usually considered medieval asceticism. To relegate fasting to antiquity is a mistake for the serious student of healing. Many people who fast regularly attest to its therapeutic power. When properly undertaken, with daily bowel irrigation to eliminate fecal poison, the fast results in a feeling of freshness and lightness, after about two days of hunger pangs. As the body frees itself of the toxicity which forms from much that we ingest, our normal healing and recreative forces function more efficiently. It is not the cure-all some claim it to be, but it is a cure-much.

Fasting (free from public display, as Jesus commanded) sensitizes one's very soul. It is as though calluses were painlessly removed from the fingertips. Feelings, awareness, and a certain deep knowing about God, ourselves, and others surface from some part of our being which fasting feeds. We allow ourselves a clearer focus on the divine. A hunger often unfelt as we eat and eat and eat draws us to the table of the Lord. We hunger for him and are satisfied.

Whether a fast has been for one day or two weeks, it should not be broken too abruptly. The longer a person fasts, the more important it is to resume eating solid foods gradually. The first foods consumed should be mild and easily digested, like chicken soup, jello, or custard. After one or two such meals, heavier foods may be consumed.

Bowel irrigation is also important. The *People's Almanac* contains a sensible, concise discussion of the hows and whys of what they term bowel bathing.

There is another aspect of fasting that may be more important than abstaining from physical food. We feed our minds daily but not wisely. We tend to be food junkies when it comes to mental diet. We are so accustomed to stuffing our minds with negative thoughts that we become inured to them and are unaware of how the unwholesome fare poisons our hearts. The New Testament charges us, "Whatsoever things are pure . . . whatsoever things are of good report, think on these things." Unless we conform to that rule, emotional health is impossible.

Fasting from negative thoughts and expressions is no easy task. It is more demanding than a food fast. My advice is to try it one day at a time. Begin anew each day. It may take a month of days, each one viewed as a fresh beginning, before a single day filled with nothing but faith and positive thought is achieved. Before you reach that point, deal gently with yourself. When negative thoughts arise, do not fight them. Gently push them out of your mind and replace them with positive thoughts. If I am confronted with the thought that April 15th will soon be here and I cannot afford to pay my income tax, for example, I just push it aside and begin to thank God for his abundance and for filling all my needs. Though not easy or automatic, mental fasting is a deeply rewarding experience. It is one more step toward the goal St. Paul taught and sought of "casting down imagination and every high thing which exalts itself against the knowledge of God and bringing into captivity every thought to the obedience of Christ."

This is not to suggest that all negative thoughts are bad any more than physical fasting implies that all food is bad. Such disciplines serve as balancing, corrective forces. When negative thoughts are brought under the mastery of our will, they can function like the negative pole of a compass. They aid in guidance and growth rather than obscure it.

A combination of fasting and prayer is a dialectic for spiritual power. Fasting empties, prayer fills; fasting purifies, prayer inspires. It is one of the relaxation/action cycles found in every living thing. It is part of the universe, the pulse beat of life. The discipline of physical and mental fasting, accompanied by faithful prayer, would deliver us from a lot of evil that stubbornly resists removal.

AUTHENTIC MODEL OF THE TEMPLE OF HEROD. Adjoining the Holy Land Hotel on a hill overlooking the new section of Jerusalem is an accurate representation of the Jerusalem of the first century, reduced in scale. Houses, public buildings, government structures, walls, towers, and divisions are portrayed in great detail with fidelity. Constructed of tiny pieces of stone, the model cost over $1 million.

THE STEPS TO THE TEMPLE AREA, JERUSALEM. Archeologists have uncovered the steps by which Jesus ascended to the Temple of Herod.

THE DOME OF THE ROCK, SITE OF HEROD'S TEMPLE, JERUSALEM. This most magnificent of Moslem temples is built upon the platform of Herod's Temple and the earlier temple of Solomon. Herod's Temple was the setting of several of Jesus' healings. The rock on which it was built is believed by some, with good reason, to be where Abraham was to sacrifice his son Isaac. Sacred to Jews, Moslems, and Christians, this place is perhaps the most revered on earth.

ST. MARK'S ORTHODOX CONVENT, JERUSALEM. Inscriptions discovered in the foundations of this ancient convent indicate that early tradition held it to be the site of the original Upper Room, where Jesus administered the Lord's Supper and where, later, the Holy Spirit came upon the first congregation of Christianity as they gathered after the Ascension.

They came to the other side of the sea, to the country of the Gerasenes. And when he had come out of the boat, there met him out of the tombs a man with an unclean spirit, who lived among the tombs; and no one could bind him any more, even with a chain; for he had often been bound with fetters and chains, but the chains he wrenched apart, and the fetters he broke in pieces; and no one had the strength to subdue him. Night and day among the tombs and on the mountains he was always crying out, and bruising himself with stones. And when he saw Jesus from afar, he ran and worshiped him; and crying out with a loud voice, he said, "What have you to do with me, Jesus, Son of the Most High God? I adjure you by God, do not torment me." For he had said to him, "Come out of the man, you unclean spirit!" And Jesus asked him, "What is your name?" He replied, "My name is Legion; for we are many." And he begged him eagerly not to send them out of the country. Now a great herd of swine was feeding there on the hillside; and they begged him, "Send us to the swine, let us enter them." So he gave them leave. And the unclean spirits came out, and entered the swine; and the herd, numbering about two thousand, rushed down the steep bank into the sea, and were drowned in the sea.

The herdsmen fled, and told it in the city and in the country. And people came to see what it was that had happened. And they came to Jesus, and saw the demoniac sitting there, clothed and in his right mind, the man who had had the legion; and they were afraid. And those who had seen it told what had happened to the demoniac and to the swine. And they began to beg Jesus to depart from their neighborhood. And as he was getting into the boat, the man who had been possessed with demons begged him that he might be with him. But he refused, and said to him, "Go home to your friends, and tell them how much the Lord has done for you, and how he has had mercy on you." And he went away and began to proclaim in the Decapolis how much Jesus had done for him; and all men marveled.

Mark 5:1–20

CHAPTER EIGHT

MEETING THE SABER LADY:

The Healing Ministry of Exorcism

The story of Jesus' encounter with a man called Legion reveals as does none other his absolute mastery over the demonic and his power to release and heal the possessed. Jesus is the protagonist in a stranger-than-fiction drama as ghoulish and terrifying as the most chilling moments of *The Exorcist*. Through the years this story has fascinated me. I have read it scores of times, imagining what the momentous clash between the divine and the satanic must have been like, and pondering what it means to us today.

Jesus jumped from the prow of the fishing boat the disciples had grounded on the Galilean beach in the area of Gadara on the sea's eastern shore. As he walked toward one of the limestone cliffs that jutted abruptly from the shoreline he heard a chilling scream. It was a man's voice, though it sounded barely human—more like the deep wail of a great wounded beast. Jesus then saw the man: like an apparition from the Inferno he stood naked, his body covered with filth-laden scabs and fresh, self-inflicted wounds; his face a mask of diabolic madness; his eyes windows into hell—wild, fearful pools of insane self-hatred.

The wild man of Gadara lived in the caves that pocked the face of the cliff. They were used as burial crypts by the local inhabitants. A suitable home for this living corpse, thought the disciples, who anxiously stood their ground. Jesus advanced toward the man until they stood only a few feet apart. The Nazarene's eyes held the gaze of the madman, and the army of the damned that occupied him knew that it was defeated by a superior force. They knew they had to obey the instructions of the Prince of Light, who looked upon human bodies as temples of the Holy Spirit and was angered when any dark power desecrated one of them. They begged Jesus not to send them away from the region, but rather to send them into the nearby grazing swine—an acceptable request, since the pigs were carriers of deadly disease and did violence to the conscience of a people whose Levitical dietary law prohibited the eating of pork.

The innocent swine, prostituted by the demons, purged themselves, cold vibrations of death sweeping over them as they stampeded over the cliff and into the sea. Jesus' spirit blessed those man-cursed creatures, for he knew that soon he would voluntarily die that men and all creation might not ever know the curse of death again.

The man once called Legion stood smiling before Jesus. Awakened from a nightmare, he knew peace for the first time in his life. He looked at Jesus, who was radiating joy and love! The released man felt like he was raised from the dead or was in heaven; whichever it was, Jesus had caused it to happen, and he never wanted to leave his presence.

Jesus instructed his amazed, bewildered disciples to bathe the man in the lake and share some of their clothing with him. When the swine herders, who had run all the way to Gadara with their strange tale, returned accompanied by some of the curious townspeople, there was the terror of the region quietly sitting at Jesus' feet, clothed and obviously very sane. The episode troubled the people. It would be better to have a few loonies around than to have a holy man threatening their livelihood. The merchants of death asked the Lord of Life to leave and never come back.

Two thousand years later we still have the demon-possessed among us. And we still have Gadarene citizens who would rather remain undisturbed than seriously consider the phenomena of possession and deliverance. Although a handful of Christians have gone to silly and sometimes destructive excesses, blaming demons for almost every problem in life, most Christians and psychologists have chosen to deny that the existence of demons has any authenticity. It would not matter that much if it were just a matter for academic debate. But it is not. St. Paul said, "We wrestle not against flesh and blood but against principalities, and powers and rulers of darkness in high places." I sympathize with the timid souls who would rather ignore the whole spooky subject. I felt the same way myself, until I became convinced that the idea of a conscious malevolent being possessing and controlling a person is more than a silly medieval myth. And it is noteworthy that the subject of possession is now taken seriously by some psychiatrists and psychologists.

"Powers and rulers of darkness" were at work in Adolf Hitler and in the other men, kind husbands and good fathers, who kissed their loved ones good-bye in the morning, traveled to the nearby concentration camps, donned their coveralls, spent their working days killing innocent people by the thousands, the millions, and then returned home to their beloved families. It takes a fanatic's gullibility to say,

"Well, that's just the way people are." That is *not* the way people are. It is an example of the demonic takeover of a society. The cases of multiple personality documented in such stories as *The Three Faces of Eve* and *Sybil* are perhaps further examples of the demonic.

One of the important ministries of the church has always been exorcism. It holds no natural attraction for me; but when it is exercised with wisdom, it has the miraculous beauty of Legion's deliverance.

I was asked by a close friend, a Presbyterian minister in my hometown of Fayetteville, what I knew about demons and exorcism. "I've run into something that sounds an awful lot like possession, and I'd like you to help," he said, when I told him I had had a few personal experiences with exorcism.

"I will if I can. What is it?" I asked.

"We've been looking into the subject of possession in a Bible class, and after one of the discussions some of the participants came to me about a woman who lives very near my church. She's a wild-eyed woman with uncombed hair down to her waist, who stands on her porch and screams at passing school kids. Sometimes, with no provocation, she throws stones at them and curses them. They say she usually walks around with a saber in her hand."

Hearing that description, I was not at all sure that I wanted to lend my assistance. Yet when he asked me if I would go with him to see this woman, I said,

"Yes, I will. But for the next week, before we go, I want you to ask your class to fast and pray."

The following week, the minister and I went to the prosperous, well-maintained house of the saber lady. When the door opened, there stood a woman who for all the world looked like the witch in *The Wizard of Oz* after a nose job. Her eyes were filled with fear. She checked the screen door to be sure it was locked before asking what we wanted. Then, before we could answer, she began to laugh—a cold, shrill cackle that made me want to run. I looked down at the infamous saber gripped tightly in her right hand.

I had counseled hundreds of people, including some violent and irrational personalities, but what this woman was sending out was something more than simply emotional illness. What the New Testament calls the gift of discernment told me that she was in fact possessed.

The minister introduced himself and then me and told her we had come to talk to her.

"I'd be glad to talk," she said. "What would you like to talk about?" But she made no move to open the locked screen door and let us in. Standing awkwardly at the doorway, we began to talk about Christ. Her involvement in the conversation was surprising. She possessed a wealth of information on the Bible, history, and religion in general. We spent over an hour at her door, peering through the screen at each other, talking a lot but going nowhere verbally or physically.

When we drew the conversation to a close the minister asked if we could return another time to continue our discussion.

"Sure, why not?" was her tentative agreement.

With our foot almost in the door we were determined to see the encounter to a redemptive conclusion. We reported back to the study group, who agreed to maintain a prayer campaign for the saber lady and we decided to return the following Monday at the same time.

On our next visit she opened the door a crack and said, "Go to the bedroom window over there," pointing a few feet to our left. Her obvious strategy, dictated by some dark paranoia, was to talk to us with all the doors securely locked.

We walked over to the window and there she stood, holding that awful saber. Her lips smiled, but her eyes glared. "How pathetic she is," I thought. "Lord, set her free." That was my prayer not only at that moment, but through almost every day, as I felt my heart embrace her. I wanted to put my arms around her and say, "Come out of your prison. Satan has no power over you. Christ died to set you free." But I knew that we had to coax her ever so slowly to the door of her infernal cell. She somehow held the key, which we prayed would be revealed by the Holy Spirit. We were determined to see her set free.

From September through mid-January, our weekly

through-the-open-window conversations continued. Finally the breakthrough came. On a snowy day, rare in the South, we stood at the window, chilled to the bone.

"I can't stand this cold very long," I said to my colleague.

He said to the saber lady, "It's very cold. May we talk inside today?"

A look of abject panic came over her face. "No, No, No!" she screamed. "Stay out. You must stay out!"

"Well, we can't stand out here like this," he said with resignation. "Ruth, why don't you lead us in the Lord's Prayer. Then we'll leave." We had never said the Lord's Prayer there before, but it seemed just right, somehow; though at that moment, I could not have said why.

"Our Father, who art in heaven, Hallowed be Thy name, Thy Kingdom come, Thy will be done, On Earth as it is in heaven. Give us this day our daily bread, And forgive us our trespasses As we forgive those who . . ."

"No, no, no, no! I will never forgive them!" she screamed at the top of her voice. "I will never forgive them. As long as I live I will never forgive . . . I'll *never* . . . Go away. Go away," she (it?) cried, "and don't come back."

She had given us the key. We had identified the demon: "My name is Unforgiveness. This fool invited me in through the gate of her unrelenting bit-

118

terness. I've done nothing but live in the wonderfully foul atmosphere her maddened mind created. I'm no intruder; I'm a welcome, able supervisor of her hateful little spirit."

"In the name of Jesus Christ, come out of her," I prayed. "The blood of Jesus, I plead the blood of my holy Savior to purge this woman's soul. Savior, let your light shine into her darkness. Oh blessed Jesus, set her free."

The woman crumpled to the floor; the saber fell from her hand. As she lay there motionless, apparently unconscious, we continued to pray for her—to pray with more than words. Our hearts embraced this fallen soul. Eventually she stood up and walked into another room, as though she did not even know we were there, as though she had just awakened from a sleep of many years. We walked to the car. I was trembling with cold and emotion and puzzled by what had happened. Was she free, or was she still cowering behind those bars of bitterness?

We did not return at the usual time the next week, honoring her command to stay away, but we prayed and waited. We finally did return several weeks later and found the house empty, which heightened our concern for her fate. Then her husband, an army officer at Fort Bragg, called to thank me and the minister for the unbelievable change in his wife. One day he had returned from work to a smiling, serene wife, a welcome transformation from the strange and emotional woman he had seen the morning before. On that day she had asked him to take her to the beauty parlor so she could get her hair fixed, and asked him if she could buy some new clothes. The shocked husband agreed enthusiastically. "And when the townspeople came to Jesus, there was Legion seated before him, clothed and in his right mind."

The once-possessed woman had one other request: she wanted to move from the house. How filled with ugly memories and emotions it must have been! Her husband applied for a transfer and they moved to a distant city.

"And deliver us from evil, For Thine is the Kingdom and the Power and the Glory. Forever and ever. Amen."

THE ROCK OF AGONY. In the Church of All Nations in Jerusalem, a great rock memorializes the agony of Jesus in the Garden of Gethsemane, on Mt. Olivet. Outside, in the garden itself, ancient olive trees are still to be seen, some of which have been dated by archeologists as possibly being from the time of Jesus.

THE GREAT OLIVE TREES IN THE GARDEN OF GETHSEMANE, JERUSALEM. Still bearing leaves and fruit, these few huge trees are vivid reminders of the time of Christ, and of his suffering here. Here, too, he prayed for all who would believe in his name.

THE FIRST PRISON OF JESUS. When Jesus was arrested in the Garden of Gethsemane, he was brought for interrogation to the home of the High Priest. In the lower part of that building, now underneath a church, is the dungeon where Jesus was held and beaten.

THE ENTRANCE TO JESUS' SECOND PRISON. Not far from the Roman Gabbatha (pavement) where Jesus was tortured is the prison of Barabbas. Jesus also may have been held here for a time.

THE ROMAN PAVEMENT BENEATH JERUSALEM. Here Jesus was beaten by the Roman guards of Pilate. On the surface of the stones are inscribed markings of a dice game played by the soldiers. The winner, called "King for a Day," was rewarded by being relieved of certain onerous duties. Jesus was mockingly called a king here, crowned with a crown of thorns, given a reed as scepter, and robed in tatters. The mocking soldiers unconsciously paid him homage, for King he surely was, both genealogically (in the succession of David) and by his divinity and Lordship.

And when Elizabeth heard the greeting of Mary, the babe leaped in her womb; and Elizabeth was filled with the Holy Spirit and she exclaimed with a loud cry, "Blessed are you among women, and blessed is the fruit of your womb!"

Luke 1:41–42

THE
LEAP
FOR
JOY:

Inner Healing Begins Early

"And when Elizabeth heard the greeting of Mary, the babe [John the Baptist] leaped in her womb. . . ." It is uncanny, this idea that an unborn baby could respond to a conversation between his Aunt Mary and his mother; that he could leap for joy when the pregnant woman who was to bear Jesus entered his mother's presence. But that is exactly what Luke the physician says happened.

This story is significant because it expresses a concept overlooked by psychology until recently: our emotional development begins in the womb, not on the day of our birth. Expectant mothers are warned by medical science that the intemperate use of alcohol, tobacco, and certain other drugs can be harmful to the unborn child. The tranquilizer Thalidomide, for example, was removed from the market when it was proved that it had caused tragic birth defects when taken by expectant mothers. Women are usually instructed by their obstetricians in proper diet and exercise to increase the likelihood of the baby's healthy development during gestation. But what must be added to even the most enlightened program of prenatal care is the importance of the emotional climate that surrounds the unborn child. No comprehensive approach to the healing and development of the whole person can ignore this area today.

When I am requested by a pregnant mother to pray for God's blessing on the baby she is carrying in her womb, I do not take lightly the request. I pray knowing that her baby is as sensitive to the flow of emotion and spiritual power generated by prayer as is the mother—perhaps more so. And whenever possible I instruct pregnant women to fill their lives with positive thoughts and experiences; these are far more important than diet or exercise. A mother's tempers and tensions can all too easily be translated into emotional trauma in her baby.

A part of the Good News, however, is that when damage is done to our emotions before birth the

Holy Spirit can take us back to the moment of trauma and injury and heal us. "He shall restore the harvest the locusts have destroyed" is the scriptural promise. Many people, unlike John, who felt the joyous surge of happy emotions in the womb, felt a cold wave of rejection as their first emotion. Even before they were born they knew they were not wanted: they felt the hate and fear of their mother or father. (Experience in taking people through inner healing has revealed, surprisingly, that the unborn infant is almost as vulnerable to the father's negativity as to the mother's.) The victims of such rejection can suffer its effects long after birth, never consciously acknowledging the contribution of prenatal trauma to their inability to cope with life. Should the origin of an individual's problems be prenatal, the best emotional therapy, if it ignores this earlier influence, will prove ineffective.

Karen, a young drug addict whom I counseled for over two years, suffered terribly from a self-hatred that allowed her almost no appreciation of her own womanhood. Together we carefully probed into her youth, seeking out root causes for her tenacious self-contempt. After I led her in verbal prayer therapy from infancy through adolescence, she experienced some relief, but that primal release which a therapist seeks eluded us still. As I always do, I prayed continually for guidance. Each person is so utterly unique that no counselor, however well trained, has sufficiently precise insights to assist an individual in the quest for wholeness without divine guidance. It is arrogance or just plain ignorance that makes us think otherwise.

After twenty-four months of growing frustration the answer to Karen's puzzling resistance to therapy finally came. I had never seriously considered the need to go back before birth, but as I sat looking into the pain-filled eyes of my young client-become-friend, I asked, "Could it be that the root cause of your problem goes back to when you were in your mother's womb? Let's see if we can find something there." I then began to pray, asking the God who knew her before she was formed in her mother's womb (Ps. 139) to carry her soul back to the time when it found residence in the womb of her mother. When I asked Jesus to hold her in his arms as she was being formed in that woman, my friend began to sob. She later told me that dark, forgotten memories began to rise in her like a diabolic flood. As I prayed that any wounding emotions from mother or father be washed away and replaced with a sense of love and acceptance, she began to writhe in uncontrollable, hysterical crying.

"She doesn't want me!" she shouted. "She doesn't want me!"

"Your mother doesn't want you?"

"Yes, oh dear God, my mother doesn't want me!"

That is all the young woman could say for some

time. After the storm of emotion began to subside, I asked her to tell me what she was experiencing.

She said, "My mother was a prostitute. Years ago she told me that she had been sleeping with several men when I was conceived, and she didn't know which one was the father. She confessed to me that I wasn't wanted, that she bitterly resented being pregnant with me."

Together we prayed that she might be reconciled to a mother who was reconceived in the daughter's heart, through faith, as a tender, loving mother.

The change in Karen was striking. In the months prior to this prayer for prenatal healing she had suffered repeated periods of depression, unable to hold down a job and lying almost pathologically. Within a short period of time she had found a job, and she began to accept my love. Soon afterward, she returned to the Midwest, where she visited her mother, and for the first time they were able to discuss freely and without malice their relationship.

It is my conviction that many of the self-destructive emotional patterns that resist psychological solution are rooted in such prenatal programming and can be uprooted and replaced by positive emotions through inner healing.

It is encouraging to know that the Holy Spirit can heal the extremely troubled, but the importance of what might be called emotional preventive medicine is undeniable. Couples should learn to make prayer a part of love, and even love-making, especially when trying to conceive a child. The husband and wife who repeatedly bless the child during its nine months of preparation for birth are contributing richly to the child's future happiness and spiritual well-being. One young expectant mother told me that when long sieges of nausea and fatigue accompanied her second pregnancy she cried and complained to herself about having "that baby" inside of her. But after her discouragement lifted somewhat, she sat and talked to the baby within her, understanding the principle of prenatal influence. Assuring the baby that she very much wanted it she would pray that Jesus would bless it and take away all the bad feelings her miserable attitude might have created. That is preventive medicine of the highest quality.

A friend once asked me, "With all the sick minds in the world, how can we ever make any appreciable advances in mental health?" It does look hopeless, I will admit. But I wonder if Thomas Edison, having invented the first incandescent light bulb, got discouraged thinking of all the lights that had to be manufactured before the whole world could be illumined. I do not think so. I think he knew that his light was so much better than the next best thing, the kerosene lamp, that each family would want *his* light. And they would want it badly enough that the wires *would* be strung and the lights *would* be made, until in homes throughout the world people would extinguish the darkness of night with his light.

In just such a way, the inner healing of Jesus Christ will one day bring mental health to the whole world. As one family after another discovers what Zechariah and Elizabeth knew, what Mary and Joseph knew, they will acknowledge the absolute importance of the soul in the womb of its mother. They will bathe the unborn child's soul in the love of Christ as parents bathe a baby's body in pure water each day after birth. They will "prepare the way of the Lord" in the heart of their child while that heart still beats in the body of the mother—a woman who, like Mary, knows that she is blessed among all women to be the mother of a child of God.

THE HILL OF THE CROSS, JERUSALEM. Jesus was crucified on a cross in front of the hill, then his body was placed in an ancient quarry bed on the flatland. The shape of a skull is clearly visible in the hill.

THE GARDEN TOMB, JERUSALEM. Located outside the north wall of Jerusalem, near the Hill of the Cross, this first-century Jewish tomb is believed by the directors of the Garden Tomb Association to be the place where Jesus was anointed and covered with the burial shroud after being taken down from the cross.

THE ENTRANCE TO THE CANOPY OF THE CHURCH OF THE HOLY SEPULCHRE IN THE BASILICA, JERUSALEM.

INSIDE THE CANOPY, CHURCH OF THE HOLY SEPULCHRE, JERUSALEM. Within the canopy is the stone slab where churchmen of the fourth century believed the body of Jesus to have been laid. The site is considered by many to be more traditional than actual.

THE CHAPEL OF THE ASCENSION, JERUSALEM. From this location, Jesus ascended to the Father in Heaven as the disciples looked on. Located on the top of the Mount of Olives, this is a frequently visited holy place.

As he passed by, he saw a man blind from his birth. And his disciples asked him, "Rabbi, who sinned, this man or his parents, that he was born blind?" Jesus answered, "It was not that this man sinned, or his parents, but that the works of God might be made manifest in him. We must work the works of him who sent me, while it is day; night comes, when no one can work. As long as I am in the world, I am the light of the world." As he said this, he spat on the ground and made clay of the spittle and anointed the man's eyes with the clay, saying to him, "Go, wash in the pool of Siloam" (which means Sent). So he went and washed and came back seeing.

John 9:1–7

MAYBE
MUD,
MAYBE
MEDICINE:

God's Prescription for Healing

Each of us is unique, our physical, emotional, and spiritual strengths and weaknesses as characteristic and identifiable as our birthmarks. Jesus was sensitive to that human individuality as he counseled, taught, and healed the sick. His response on every occasion was tailored to the needs of the person to whom he ministered.

The numerous miracle stories of the New Testament reveal variations in Jesus' healing procedure. In his encounter with the man blind from birth Jesus "spat on the ground and made clay of the spittle and anointed the man's eyes with the clay, saying to him, 'Go, wash in the pool of Siloam.' "

When the people of Bethsaida brought a blind man to Jesus, begging him to touch the man as they had perhaps seen him touch and heal others, Jesus first led him out of the village. He may have felt an atmosphere of antagonism there that had to be eliminated. He spat in the man's eyes and laid his hands on him. Vision only partially restored, Jesus placed his hands on the man's eyes, and then he "saw everything clearly."

The healing process of the blind beggar Bartimaeus is different from the two previous stories, except for the outcome. A great crowd had gathered to watch Jesus' departure from Jericho. Among them was Bartimaeus, who had heard of Jesus' claim to be the Messiah, the son of David, and believed. He shouted to Jesus who, hearing the desperate emotion in the plea, called Bartimaeus to him. A simple sentence, "Go your way, your faith has made you well," restored his sight.

What explanation is there for the different methods of healing in these and other stories? Faith is what heals on the purest, highest level. Why then the mud? Why the spittle? Why the washing in the pool? The Holy Spirit knew that physical signs would aid the evolution of the faith of the person healed. Bartimaeus, who needed no physical catalyst, stepped directly into the healing stream which flowed between Jesus' soul and his. But where the faith of others was not so strong, or where a lesson in obedience or cleansing was needed, love made allowances for those imperfections in faith. Jesus came to teach mankind the highest way, but he did not scorn lower ways if they led ultimately to the highest.

One area of healing significantly absent from Jesus' ministry is *materia medica,* the science of physical medicine. Some have interpreted its absence as proof that it has no place in Christian healing. Secular humanism, on the other hand, contends that medical science is the one and only enlightened means of healing. Neither of these views, when held to the exclusion of the other, is consistent with Jesus' concern for each individual's needs and limitations. Our society has an unbalanced, unhealthy trust in the ability of medicine and surgery to heal, but this does not lessen their validity if they are brought under the guidance of God.

Someone once likened the human body to a stringed instrument. Sometimes the strings become too slack, sometimes they become too taut; either condition brings the disharmony which is disease. Whatever best returns the strings to their proper state, whatever brings harmony, is healing. That can range from mountain air, bathing, massage, herbs, medicine, and surgery, on the physical level, to the queen of healing forces—love. God has provided various tools for returning our bodies to wholeness. He will choose mud, medicine, or the word of faith, depending on what we need and are able to accept.

The disciple of divine healing must learn that to be an effective channel of healing one must never anticipate God's prescription. Dr. Paul Tournier, noted Christian psychiatrist, describes in his book *The Meaning of Persons* how he learned this lesson. A patient with an emotional problem came to him for help and was treated successfully. So when another person with the same condition came to Dr. Tournier for counseling and treatment, he used the same approach, step by step, as that which had produced success in the earlier patient. To his dismay, the second patient did not respond to his therapy as the first one had. This failure led to the valuable discovery that he must pray for divine guidance before counseling with each patient. When he got on his knees in the privacy of his inner office and asked for the Holy Spirit's direction, the frequency of his success in counseling increased sharply. He learned never to anticipate what a patient needed. God knew; he did not. He became a better doctor when he learned to depend on God's knowledge.

Norman Cousins, former editor of *Saturday Review*, gained a similar understanding when he was faced with a terminal illness. He shared that understanding in an article in the *New England Journal of Medicine*.

Shortly after returning from a cultural exchange in Russia, he was incapacitated by a disease destroying his connective tissue. His personal physician of many years told him that the condition was incurable. He was hospitalized, in constant pain and unable to move any part of his body.

Cousins remembered having read a paper written by a German physician on the relationship of emotional trauma to a wide spectrum of disease. Negative emotions had been found to cause pancreatic shock, which in turn triggered the diseased condition. Cousins concluded that if negative emotions could cause disease, pleasant emotions must stimulate health. He believed in prayer, as he indicated in the article, but he wanted some way to induce happy emotions.

He asked for permission to make some changes in his care and treatment, and, because he and his doctor had been friends for many years, permission was granted. He was transferred from the hospital to a pleasant hotel room, free of the oppressive atmosphere he had felt at the hospital. He contacted Allen Funt, creator of the television show "Candid Camera," requesting that Funt send him some of his funnier half-hour programs. His nurse was given instructions on projector operation, and the treatment was under way. After Cousins watched a "Candid Camera" segment, his blood sedimentation test, a crucial indicator of his condition, was significantly improved. The half hour of laughter produced freedom from pain for almost three hours, and he could sleep without sedation. His experimental remedy also included daily doses of seven to ten grams of intravenous vitamin C. His doctor questioned the wisdom of such high vitamin consumption, but Cousins reminded him that if he was medically hopeless, the unconventional treatment could not worsen his prognosis.

In a matter of weeks Cousins was up and around, able to work in his office for a few hours each day. Soon he was totally recovered. His home remedy, with all the earmarks of divine guidance, had healed him. But his wise comment at the conclusion of his story is that this was a cure for his particular condition. He makes no claim for others.

Dr. Carl Simonton, formerly chief radiologist at Travis Air Force Base in California, became discouraged over his low success rate in the cure of cancer patients through conventional radiation treatment and chemotherapy—less than ten percent. He began to interview cancer patients whose prognosis had been terminal and who had ceased treatment but who, surprisingly, had lived. In Portland, Oregon, he questioned over 100 cancer victims whose carcinoma had gone into total remission for no clinically definable reason. When asked how they were cured, they gave many different explanations, some believable, others not. One element was present in all the accounts, however. In each case, a radical change in attitude from negative to positive had occurred sometime between the discovery of their cancer and their healing.

Dr. Simonton then began to investigate various attitude-changing methods and activities. He spent a year at the Stanford Research Institute looking into such techniques as biofeedback and hypnosis and found them inadequate. Then, back in Portland, he learned of a class in meditation being taught at the Y.M.C.A. With strong reservations he enrolled. In that eight-week course, he later admitted, he learned more about attitude changing than in his year at Stanford.

Dr. Simonton's next discovery was that every cancer patient, of those who submitted to their psychometry and analysis, showed a strong but unconscious will to die. Usually this was traced to an emotional trauma which had occurred six months to a year before the discovery of the cancer.

Piecing together the parts, he arrived at a startling conclusion: cancer is emotionally induced. It is the cautious judgment of leading cancer research programs that cancer is caused by carcinogenic bacteria. But what makes one person immune and another susceptible may be, as Dr. Simonton believes, the will (usually totally unconscious) to die. As the will to live breaks down, so too does the body immune system, permitting the bacteria to successfully in-

vade the body and destroy normal cellular development.

In collaboration with his wife, a psychologist, he
combines meditation, prayer visualization, and individual and group psychotherapy into a tool for healing cancer. Is it valid? Look at the record. He now has
a success rate of over eighty percent, as opposed to
ten percent with conventional cancer therapy. Is it
Christian? As Christian as penicillin, computers, or
jet planes. They all work; whether or not they are
Christian just depends on whether or not we take the
medicine, use the computer, or ride the airplane to
Christ's glory. They are all effective because they
follow divine laws. In that sense they are directly
from the hand of God, and by their nature honor
him.

A Christian can arrive at a mathematical conclusion by counting on fingers, mentally referring to a
memorized mathematical table, using an abacus,
feeding the question into a computer, or relying on
spiritual intuition. The latter is the highest way, but
all are valid. The best way for us as individuals depends on our own particular level. The same principle holds true in the healing of the body and mind.
We must seek the highest way, which is pure faith
healing. But that demands an individual and collective faith rarely found in our doubt-plagued society
So, just as Jesus used mud and water on sightless eyes
—nothing more than a "visualizing" process for a

blind man incapable of realizing healing by faith alone—we can use medicine, psychology, faith-imagination, or any other method which is in harmony with Christ's love. Some of these methods may seem strange and threatening to old-wineskin minds. But they are a part of the new wine of the Spirit God is now pouring out on all flesh.